# SUPER
## SEARCHERS
# DO BUSINESS

**The Online Secrets of
TOP BUSINESS RESEARCHERS**

# SUPER
## SEARCHERS
# DO BUSINESS

**The Online Secrets of
TOP BUSINESS RESEARCHERS**

## Mary Ellen Bates
### Edited by Reva Basch

CyberAge Books

*Second printing,* June 2000

**Super Searchers Do Business**

Super Searchers, Volume I
A series edited by Reva Basch

*Liability*
The opinions of the searchers being interviewed are their own and not necessarily those of their employers, the author, editor or publisher. Information Today, Inc. does not guarantee the accuracy, adequacy, or completeness of any information and is not responsible for any errors or omissions or the results obtained from the use of such information.

*Trademarks*
Trademarks and service names have been used throughout this book. The names are used with capitalization in the style used by the name claimant. The exception is the use of the trademarked name "LISTSERV." Many of the searchers being interviewed used this term generically and their usage has been retained in this book. Rather than insert a trademark notation at each occurrence of the name, the publisher states that all such trademarks are used in an editorial manner without any intent to infringe upon the trademark.

### Library of Congress Cataloging-in-Publication Data

Bates, Mary Ellen.
    Super searchers do business : the online secrets of top business
researchers / by Mary Ellen Bates.
       p.         cm.
    Includes bibliographical references and index.
    ISBN 0-910965-33-1 (pbk.)
    1. Business--Research--Methodology.   2. Electronic information
resource searching.    I. Title.
HD30.4.B377    1999
025.06'65--dc21

                                             99-21689
                                                CIP

ISBN 0-910965-33-1

Printed and bound in the United States of America

Managing Editor: Dorothy J. Pike
Cover Designer: Jacqueline Walter
Book Designer: Patricia F. Kirkbride
Indexer: Sharon Hughes

# Dedication

To my family:
Flo and Pete Bates,
Amy Grant,
Sarah Van de Wetering,
and Russell Bates,
and—always—to Dave.

# About The Super Searchers Web Page

At the Information Today Web site, you will find *The Super Searchers Web Page*, featuring links to sites mentioned in this book. We will periodically update the page, removing dead links and adding additional sites that may be useful to readers.

*The Super Searchers Web Page* is being made available as a bonus to readers of *Super Searchers Do Business* and other books in the Super Searchers series. To access the page, an Internet connection and Web browser are required. Go to:

## www.infotoday.com/supersearchers

# Table of Contents

# Foreword

In 1991, the year *Secrets of the Super Searchers* was conceived, the last of the *Indiana Jones* movies was still echoing in my head. I imagined the title swooping across the cover of my as-yet-unborn book in three-dimensional letters, like the saga of that larger-than-life hero. It was all going to be very dramatic—a multi-hero book, with tales of high-speed pursuit, clever evasive tactics, narrow escapes from crushing Dialog bills, and hidden treasures triumphantly revealed. No snakes, probably—but you never know.

The power of that first book lay in its first-person narratives, the individual voices of librarians, independent researchers, subject specialists and end users of information in fields ranging from business and finance to journalism, chemistry, engineering, patents, and medicine. Each spoke vividly and enthusiastically about what he or she knew best: how to conceive and execute a research project; how to get the most out of the available online tools; the tricks, tips and cost-shaving shortcuts learned from a career's worth of interaction with the industrial-strength, pay-for-the-privilege, professional online services.

Its 1996 successor, *Secrets of the Super Net Searchers*, documented the many ways in which online searchers were integrating Internet and Web searching into their professional toolkits. In retrospect, this second book seems like an extravagantly ambitious effort—confronting and assimilating not only a greatly expanded definition of "online," but also the effects of a sudden abundance of computer-fluent end users, which was further complicated by the degree to which the Net had penetrated and was in the process of transforming individual subject disciplines. Nor could we ignore the new and vastly more complicated questions surrounding intellectual property and the quality and reliability of information. If I *were* in the movie business, I'd be tempted to call *Super Net Searchers* "breathtaking in its scope and grandeur."

When John Bryans of Information Today, Inc. first approached me with the idea of editing a series of "Super Searcher" books, I thought, "Too weird. I'm being branded." But my healthy ego saw me through that initial, squeamish reaction, and the more I thought about it, the more sense it made. We'd gone broad, publishing two successful books that attempted to encompass the universe of online research as it existed at the time from the perspective of a group of expert practitioners. But the online world had grown far beyond a generalist approach. Following the same path and publishing a *Return of the Super Searchers* in 1999 would have meant packaging a high-power magnifier with a thick, microtext-printed volume—*The Compact Oxford English Super Searchers*, perhaps? No, it was clearly time to go deep—to focus on key areas of practice within the online research profession and to unpack and expand upon the knowledge intrinsic to each one.

I first met Mary Ellen Bates in 1991 or '92, around the time that the first Super Searchers book was gestating in my mind. Neither of us can recall the exact circumstances. It may have been at an annual conference of the Association of Independent Information Professionals, or at an informal meeting of AIIPers organized by Linda Cooper at a Philadelphia restaurant. Mary Ellen served as president of AIIP—a definite bonding experience—several years after I did. We've shared the podium at professional meetings (and toyed with the idea of taking our sister act on the road) and occupied the identical conference keynote slots in consecutive years. We've edited each other's books— two apiece, by my count, including this one—and discovered in the process that we suffer fools to exactly the same degree. I know for a fact that we both play Grateful Dead tapes while we're working, wore Birkenstocks way before they were cool, and consider Northern California our spiritual home. I graciously overlook the fact that she is a dog person whereas I am privileged to live with cats. Mary Ellen and I sometimes joke that we're on the same career trajectory—only I get to retire before she does.

A book on business searching was the logical choice to kick off this new Super Searchers series. I began my own checkered career as an online searcher in an engineering library and moved on to deal with medical, legal, and patent searching as well as the cross-disciplinary free-for-all that was our daily fare in the research department at Information on Demand. But business searching in its various manifestations—company and industry backgrounders, competitive intelligence, market research and so on—has always been the core of my professional practice. It's the language I speak most fluently, the territory where I'm most at home.

I know that's true for Mary Ellen as well. In fact, she is the quintessential business researcher. Her knowledge of specialized sources and techniques, both online and off-line, runs deep, swift, and—no pun intended—current. In the last couple of years, I've extricated myself from the day-to-day fray of reference interviewing, search strategizing, running queries through the appropriate selection of databases and search engines, and analyzing and post-processing the results. Mary Ellen is still in the trenches, though, working alongside her professional colleagues—librarians, independent "informationists," and informed end-user clients—finding the answers, offering solutions, and keeping an eye on the shifting landscape of new information products and services. From the sidelines, I applaud her. She's a fine writer, an incisive and insightful interviewer, and a treasured friend. I can think of no one better qualified to write this book.

Each of us is the hero of our own movie, or so the New Age truism goes. If that's the case, my *Indiana Jones* inspiration wasn't so far-fetched after all. Not only does every Super Searcher have a personal saga to relate, but every Super Searcher *book* reflects clearly the social, professional and technological issues and assumptions with which its heroes grapple and that shape their lives. As in any good movie sequel, the lead characters remain consistently competent, cool and engaging while demonstrating their ability to cope with new, unforeseen and ever-accelerating challenges. In the best sequels, the heroes show personal growth as well; they become a little less starry-eyed—and a bit more cynical, perhaps—but always resourceful, willing to take risks, unafraid of whatever the next plot twist might bring.

The first wave of Super Searchers were secure in their role as information intermediaries, working with a demanding but well-defined universe of online databases and professional research services. The second wave had begun to cope with the realization that their world was changing; the Net had arrived, and their comfortable but circumscribed realm of expertise would never be quite the same again. Now, with *Super Searchers Do Business* and its cast of tens, our heroes are at home in this new, totally transformed, and essentially unbounded information environment. They're making the rules. They're reinventing themselves and redefining their competencies as research professionals. They're extending their reach and that of all researchers and ensuring our continued relevance—our survival—in the crazy and unpredictable age of the Web.

Thanks to Mary Ellen's skill as an interviewer and her subjects' charm, eloquence and expertise, each of these eleven interviews is fascinating in its own way. You'll laugh; you'll nod in recognition; you'll shake your head in sympathy; you'll learn something from each one. These *are* dramatic stories—even without snakes.

Reva Basch
The Sea Ranch, California
April 1999

# Acknowledgments

First, I must acknowledge the incredible generosity of the Super Searchers profiled in this book. Without them this book could not exist. I enjoyed each interview and learned something new from every one of them. Bob, Anne, Linda, Helene, Susan, Seymour, Tom, Elizabeth, Bruce, Jan and Grace—thank you for making this book possible.

Also intimately involved in the interview process was Patty Shannon of The Work Station, who transcribed these interviews quickly and accurately. She managed to catch all the obscure industry acronyms and keep up with fast-paced conversations. Her phonetic spellings of the few names that eluded her were clear and easy to decipher.

Reva Basch—friend, colleague and executive editor—has been her usual calm, supportive, unflappable self. Her suggestions have always been thoughtful, her input always valuable. I was flattered when she approached me about working on this continuation of the Super Searcher series, particularly since I found both *Secrets of the Super Searchers* and *Secrets of the Super Net Searchers* to be so valuable. Her guiding hand in this book has been, as usual, a tremendous asset.

I had the pleasure of working with John Bryans, editor in chief, on my first book, *The Online Deskbook*, and I was delighted to be able to work with him on this book as well. He is unfailingly enthusiastic and encouraging, and working with him is a pleasure. Dorothy Pike, managing editor, has worked to bring this book to print; I've known Dorothy for years and always enjoy the chance to work with her.

On a personal note, I want to thank Christine Henry, Carol McGee and Lisa Towne. We have been running together every weekend for close to a year now, and their encouragement and support are what enabled me to run my first marathon in October 1998. Thanks, ladies—I couldn't have done it without you.

And finally, thanks to the whole Grateful Dead family, who are carrying on the music and the soul of the greatest sound on earth.

> *Stood upon a mountain top*
> *Walked barefoot in the snow*
> *Gave the best we had to give*
> *How much we'll never know*
> —Robert Hunter & Jerry Garcia

Mary Ellen Bates
Washington, DC
April 1999

# Introduction

I remember when Reva Basch wrote the original Super Searchers book, *Secrets of the Super Searchers* (1993, Information Today, Inc.). I had the book autographed by as many of the Super Searchers as I could, and I pored over the interviews, thinking, "So *that's* how they do it!" "Wow, even Super Searchers have trouble doing that." Back then, the professional online services were our only real electronic information resource—the Net wasn't even mentioned as an alternative. Just three years later, Reva completed *Secrets of the Super Net Searchers* (1996, Information Today, Inc.), and what a difference those few years made. We were struggling with the familiar issues of integrating Internet resources into our collection of tools, grappling with the questions of reliability and retrievability, and figuring out what to watch for as the Web evolved into the multimedia resource that it is.

What I find interesting as I reflect back on those two Super Searchers books is that a few years ago it was at least possible to think in terms of professional online services *or* the Net. The information environment was still divided into the high-cost, value-added services such as Dialog, Dow Jones and Lexis-Nexis on the one hand and the free-for-the-taking material on the Internet on the other.

By 1999, it seems that we have an entirely new set of challenges. We're seeing a tremendous blurring of the lines between the free resources on the Internet and the professional online services. A number of Net-based, hybrid online services are offering high-quality information for a small fee or for a flat yearly fee. The professional online services are making their systems accessible directly through the Web in addition to the traditional access methods such as a dial-up, plain ASCII, command-line connection through telnet or a packet-switched network.

More information providers on the Web are now beginning to charge for what previously had been either free or not available electronically at all. Some government resources—the STAT-USA database produced by the U.S. Department of Commerce comes to mind—reflect the entrance of taxpayer-supported information sources into the competitive world of fee-based information. Associations are using the Web to promote their publications and are providing private areas in which additional material may be made available to dues-paying members only.

The proliferation of company Web sites means that business researchers have access to a wealth of information that was difficult or impossible to find in the past. Electronic discussion groups and the searchable archives of those discussions have opened up entirely new areas of business research. Online professionals are using the discussion groups as a networking tool, a way to find out about an obscure or newly introduced information resource, and a source for news of the information industry in general.

Our challenge now is to sort through what David Curle of Outsell, Inc. (www.outsellinc.com) calls "content spaghetti." He is referring to the phenomenon in which an information vendor makes its product available through a number of channels—as a discrete database on Dialog or Lexis-Nexis, as an unbranded collection of material on Dow Jones Interactive, as a site-licensed product delivered directly to a client's intranet, as a product searchable directly on the vendor's Web site, and as content included within a Web search engine such as Northern Light.

On the other hand, it's significantly easier to talk with searchers about how they find information today than it was a few years ago. When Reva was interviewing her Super Net Searchers, the Web was just beginning to come into its own. Searchers were trying to figure out how to best and most efficiently use ftp, gopher, telnet and the Web. The entire information environment felt like it was evolving at some terribly accelerated pace—dog years come to mind. By 1999, the Web has become ensconced as the primary protocol for navigation and dissemination of information on the Internet. There are new multimedia applications, new versions of HTML, even the development of Internet II. But the *rate* of fundamental change in how we navigate the Internet seems to have slowed down significantly. Thus, searchers can focus their attention on the content and searchability of information rather than worry about the protocol through which the information is made available.

So now we can start asking Super Searchers the content-specific questions: How do you find information on business-related topics? How do you integrate the value-added information services and the Net-based information into your search strategies? Do your clients, patrons, users expect you to find everything you need on the Net? For that matter, are they doing their own business research on the Web? What impact has that had on your searching?

The people whose insights are included in this book are business researchers with varied backgrounds. You will hear from a business investigator, a competitive intelligence expert, a business valuation expert, corporate librarians and independent information professionals. There are views from the vendor's perspective as well as from the user's. There are people with master's degrees in library science and professionals who are entirely self-taught in research and online skills. Without exception, the searchers use both the Net and the more traditional online sources for their business research, although the percentage to which they rely on one or the other varies significantly.

*Super Searchers Do Business* consists of eleven interviews with researchers and information professionals who understand how to get the most out of their search efforts and who can describe the tricks and techniques they rely on to uncover the best information possible. Many have backgrounds in library science; all are proficient in both Net searching and the use of the more traditional online services such as Dow Jones or Dialog. They know what they like and aren't afraid to talk about what they don't like in the online world.

The hardest challenge I had when beginning this book was deciding who, among all the expert business researchers I know and know of, I would interview. I selected as broad a variety of people as I could, in terms of their experience, their focus, and their background. Interestingly, virtually all of them got into online research as a second career or profession. Back in the 1970s, when I graduated from college with my newly minted BA in philosophy, the furthest thing from *my* mind was that I would be sitting in front of a computer all day, researching everything from the plastics industry in Belgium to municipal sewage sludge in Utah. But, like all the searchers in this book, I became attracted to the challenge of finding information, the thrill of the hunt, that *frisson* of excitement when I finally located the elusive answer to a difficult research problem. So, like many of them, I changed careers, got my master's degree in library science, and have been in the information profession ever since.

Of course, when I was in graduate school, most of our programming was done on keypunch cards, and online searching was done with an acoustic coupler, a 300-baud connection, and a thermal printer rather than a nice 17-inch monitor. Most business research was done manually—this was back before the introduction of the first PC-based spreadsheet program, after all.

The changes in the scope and depth of information available electronically have made business research both easier and more complex. It's certainly easier to get copies of annual reports, financial statements, articles from obscure business publications, and market research reports. But it's also much harder to know when you've conducted a reasonably thorough search. Gone are the days when a search of five files in Dialog, a call to a company's investor relations department and a scan of a printed index of business publications constituted an adequate job. Now we check company Web sites, look to see who has linked *to* those Web sites, search a far wider variety of online databases, consult federal and state public records on the Web, and then provide analysis and synthesis of the material. Whew! It takes a lot more to be a Super Searcher these days.

I have included traditional librarians—the original information intermediaries—in this book, as well as information business owners and "end users." I should, perhaps, explain these three categories in a little more detail. Librarians have been using online information sources for over twenty years, and were among the first to take advantage of the possibilities of the Internet. Librarians who work outside public libraries and schools are often referred to as special librarians—"special" referring to the specialized nature of their library's focus. Special librarians work in for-profit companies, for associations and nonprofit groups, in research labs and the government, in universities and in law firms. One of the major professional associations for these librarians is the Special Libraries Association (SLA); a number of the people interviewed in this book refer to electronic discussion lists of the various interest groups within SLA. Seymour Satin, Helene Kassler and Susan Klopper are all special librarians.

Also interviewed were independent information professionals—people who own their own businesses and who provide research and analysis to clients for a fee. Many of these independent info pros worked in libraries before they went independent;

some came to this profession after having provided research in some other capacity. Jan Tudor, Linda Cooper, Grace Villamora, Elizabeth Swan and Bruce Tincknell fall into the category of independent info pros.

My third category of Super Searchers is what I call "end users." This is another phrase that comes up frequently in interviews and has several meanings. The end-user Super Searchers I interviewed are people who conduct research, or who teach or write about it, for themselves rather than for a client or library patron. These include Tom Sterner, who provides research in conjunction with business investigations; Robert Berkman, a writer and editor of information industry publications who conducts research in conjunction with his writing; and Anne Caputo, a Dow Jones Interactive employee whose focus is the information professional community and who is also an adjunct professor in a graduate-level library science program.

Note that the phrase "end users" also appears in many of the interviews in this book. It usually refers to people who use online information sources—both free Web-based resources and the high-priced information services—for their own research. These end users are usually not trained online researchers, but are proficient at conducting basic research themselves. Often an end user will do some initial online searching and then go to a librarian or independent info pro for more in-depth research.

Although, as expected, there was a wide variety of opinions among the experts I interviewed about the best sources to use and the best techniques for finding information, there were a number of continuing themes. The following is a summary of what I heard time and again during my interviews.

## Curiosity

The Super Searchers I interviewed are people who like finding answers, who like pushing their limits, and who enjoy the thrill of the hunt as they discover new ways to find information. They—I should say "we" because I share these qualities—like the intellectual challenge of uncovering the answer. They recognize that, even though a question is similar to one they had a week ago, it may not necessarily entail the same research technique or the same sources. The client or patron is different, the parameters are different, the information environment may have shifted, their selection of resources may have changed. Several searchers described themselves as excitement junkies—they like using their creativity and they enjoy the challenge of seeing if they really can find exactly the information needed by the client within the budget and time frame allowed. In fact, sometimes it's not even finding the answer per se that proves so rewarding, but discovering the nuances of the answer and the additional *questions* that have come out of that answer. A perhaps-inevitable corollary of this is that the frustrations mentioned most frequently were the boredom of doing a project that simply isn't challenging and the difficulties of searching the Net—that is, when the technology gets in the way of our finding the answer.

## Point A to Point B via Point C

The search process itself tends to be roundabout rather than direct; very few searchers start with the same sources for every project. Instead, they use an iterative process, trying one source, seeing what turns up, trying another source, maybe going back to the first source again based on what was found along the line, and so on. They switch back and forth between the free areas on the Net and the high-priced professional online services. (Thank goodness we've moved beyond the bad old days when every online search system required its own proprietary software and we were constantly switching software as well as online systems!) Many searchers also rely on some kind of preliminary search, which gives them a sense of the parameters of the available information;

they then get back to the client to clarify, narrow or expand the research question.

## Added Value

The role of researchers—both within organizations and as independent entrepreneurs—has changed significantly over the past few years. The days of the infamous "rip and ship," when we simply ripped the search results off the printer and shipped them to a client, are gone. Just as the world is full of frustrated would-be comedians, so the business world is full of people who believe that anyone with a computer can provide high-quality research. The way to address this underestimation of the skills required to provide business research is to promote the added value that researchers can provide. Several searchers mentioned that they go out of their way to think like their clients—reading the same newspapers, attending the same conferences, and taking other steps to understand ahead of time the context from which the research projects arise. Interestingly, some of the independent info pros in this book tried to take on more entrepreneurial roles within companies before they struck out on their own—marketing the services of their information center, developing new products to market to clients, and working more closely with the company's clients.

## Analysis

One of the sentences that has stuck in my head since my interview with Linda Cooper was her comment, "I am my own end user." She explains this in chapter three, of course, but I will take the liberty of commenting here as well. Her point was that she no longer sees herself as merely the agent for her client, doing the search and handing off the results. Instead, she is finding that what her clients want is not *search results* but *research answers*. No longer content with a collection of articles or reports, they want an executive summary, a single spreadsheet with the numbers they are looking for, a PowerPoint presentation with the information in bulleted format. Researchers are being asked to do more than find the information; now we need to be able to tell our clients *why* and *how* this information answers the question. Survival in the business setting, according to our searchers, will depend on providing a high service level and on processing information to make it useful and, to use a current business buzzword, actionable.

## Reference Interviews

"User needs analysis," "reference interview" or "client wish list"—whatever it's called, searchers invariably mentioned the interview process as one of the most important parts of their research. This is often how they determine which information sources to use, how much time and budget to allocate to the project, and what additional analysis to provide. Indeed, the reference interview process itself is often an added service for the clients—it can help them define the information needed, recognize what they are in fact looking for, and think through what information they already have.

## Knowing When to Say When

Related to the reference interview is the notion of how searchers know when to end a search. Again and again, their answer was "The reference interview will have told me when I should stop." In some situations, they have used up the time and budget allotted for the project. In others, their experience and intuition tells them that they have hit all of the most likely information sources. Based on the initial needs analysis, they know whether or not a given project calls for a no-holds-barred search or a quick preliminary look. As Linda Cooper said, it's often a matter of stopping when you feel that you've come full circle and are seeing the same sources again and again. The challenge, though, is that, with the resources of the Web, it's a lot harder to make that full circle. This often comes back to the gut instinct of an experienced researcher. After a while you just *know* that you've hit the most likely sources or, more frustrating, you just *know* that there's something out there on the topic but you haven't found it yet.

## Impact of the Net on Searchers

Perhaps not surprisingly, the Super Searchers I spoke with said that the Internet has had a very positive impact on their profession. No longer do researchers see blank looks when they tell someone, "I do online research." People now understand what online information is. They realize that the Net is a largely unfiltered, unordered collection of both tremendously valuable material and useless dreck, and they recognize that it takes more than a few keystrokes to find the information they need.

On the other hand, researchers are finding that they need to check the Net even if they think that the search will be fruitless, just to avoid a client saying, as Tom Sterner puts it, "By the way, I found this on the Internet while I was watching TV. Did you find it too?" Online searchers have always known that two expert searchers will never retrieve exactly the same material when doing similar searches. That phenomenon is magnified on the Web, where not only are there many search engines to use, but the chances of retrieving the same material twice are so small. It is quite likely that the Web sites found by two Super Searchers would not overlap at all. As a result, it is often the case that a searcher will not turn up a Web site discovered by a client.

One of the ongoing concerns of Super Searchers is the need to continually remind their clients, patrons, and colleagues to think critically about what's on the Net. Data integrity is a big concern, particularly when compared to the more traditional information sources such as consulting reports, published articles in the trade and business press, and government filings. Subsequent retrievability of material found on Web sites is another concern. If a business decision or a legal argument is based on information drawn from a Web site, the researcher runs the risk of relying on material that may disappear without notice.

A welcome change noted by several of the Super Searchers is that the projects they're working on now are more complex than they used to be. Their clients, patrons or constituents are often doing their own basic research—looking through a competitor's Web site, reviewing SEC documents, and reading press releases. Now they want the researcher to find the *rest* of what's available. That makes searching a lot more interesting, but it also takes away those easy milk runs that were sometimes a nice break during the day.

## How Searchers Use the Net

The Super Searchers commented that the Net offers new information sources; it does not supplant the traditional ones. Searchers usually go to specific verified sites on the Net—tables from the U.S. Bureau of the Census, collections of press releases, and known company Web sites, for example. Search engines themselves are seen as somewhat mysterious black boxes. While it is critical to understand how each search engine works, searchers are finding it more and more difficult to suss out what exactly is going on behind the scenes: How frequently is the index refreshed; in other words, when's the last time this search engine made the rounds of the Net? Exactly how is it ranking the retrieved sites? Is one site listed first because it's most relevant or because the Web designer has fooled the search engine into ranking it first? Was the search done on exactly the words I typed or did the search engine expand the search to related concepts as well? Two of the resources frequently cited by the Super Searchers interviewed were the Search Engine Watch site and Greg Notess' columns and presentations at conferences. Keeping up with search engine developments is time-consuming and frustrating; most searchers

rely on the experts to review and evaluate search engine performance. Despite the proliferation of search engines, most searchers
use the same several they are familiar with—the ones they know,
trust and can use to best advantage.

Helene Kassler describes how she works backward from a Web
site to see what other sites are linked to it—a technique that can
yield intriguing information for competitive intelligence searchers.
As she points out, the information gleaned from this technique
would have been virtually impossible to find before the Web.

One ongoing concern of researchers is the currency of information they find on Web sites. Several said that they contact the Web
manager to get additional information on the material available on
the Web site and to verify the reliability of the information. This, it
appears, is the price we pay for free, unmediated data on the Web—
we have to function as our own fact-checkers and editors rather
than relying on the vetting normally done by publishers and editors.

One distressing trend I noticed—and this was evident in *Secrets
of the Super Net Searchers* as well—was the reluctance of most
Super Searchers to participate in the electronic discussion groups of
information professionals. The most common complaints were that
these electronic forums take far too much time to keep up with and
that there is simply too much chatter and irrelevant material on
most discussion groups. I think this is a real shame.

I remember my first introduction to electronic communities, The
WELL (www.well.com). It was, and still is, a tremendously vibrant
place, full of friendly voices, helpful and encouraging colleagues,
and a place to get to know leaders in any number of fields. Yes, there
are catfights and squabbles, just as in any large family, but all in all I
can still tap into the knowledge of experts from around the world.

Unfortunately, I too am seeing a change in the texture and quality of discussions in many of the public electronic discussion groups.
The more experienced members of the community seem to be with-
drawing, or at least reverting to read-only mode. The number of

beginner-level queries and requests for help *before* the requester has done any work herself seems to have increased. I can only encourage the rest of us information professionals to come back and join in the discussion, to add our voices—our hard-earned wisdom and valued perspective—to the mix. Yes, it's time-consuming, but hearing from other experienced info pros is what stimulates new ideas and raises discussions to a higher level.

Finally, a few notes about how this book is arranged. I remember that I read the first two Super Searchers books in bits and pieces, if for no other reason than that I found each interview to be rich in insights and full of ideas on new ways to approach searching. Trying to sit down and read the entire book straight through would have been like trying to eat my way through a dessert buffet table. I probably wouldn't have been able to do it (although it would've been fun to try!), and I would not have been able to appreciate the different flavors and textures of each item. So, I read one or two Super Searcher interviews at a time, depending on my inclination and whatever was currently puzzling me about online searching. This gave me the time to digest and think through the insights of each searcher, and an opportunity to decide which of their techniques I could adopt myself.

I thought about how to order the interviews in this book, knowing that some people may want to read them sequentially and some may skip from one to another. I could have organized the chapters by type of searcher—corporate librarian, end user, and independent info pro. Alternatively, I could have tried to find commonality among various searchers and organized them that way—those who focus on Net-based resources, those who prefer the traditional online services, those who write or teach about online searching, for example. Somehow, neither of these approaches really made sense to me.

Instead, I opted for a more intuitive approach, putting the chapters in an order that seemed to me to flow from one to the next. I

remember hearing a panel of searchers at a professional conference equating the search process to improvisational jazz. You hear
a riff, you pick it up and see where it goes, you find a similar
motif somewhere else. I felt something similar as I was interviewing these Super Searchers. I heard an idea here, heard it
repeated there, then heard it modified later. As you read these
chapters, I know you will recognize some riffs, adopt others, and
reflect on still others.

For the sake of readability, we did not include in the text the full
Internet addresses for sites mentioned in the interviews. Instead, we
have compiled all the resources described by our searchers in a single Resources section in the appendix and have noted the first mention of a resource in each chapter. This section includes Internet and
other online resources, electronic discussion groups, indispensable
reference books and magazines, and other sources. (I have taken the
risk of appearing to depersonalize a respected colleague by including Greg Notess in the list of resources. His name came up several
times as the final word in search engine content and reliability, and
he truly is one of our industry's valuable resources.) We eliminated
the "http://" from the beginning of Internet addresses; this is yet
another indication that the Net has settled down somewhat and the
industry seems to have agreed on a standard protocol for the distribution of information via the Net.

We have also included a brief glossary in the appendix, listing
TLAs (three-letter acronyms) and other terms and phrases used by
our interviewees. It is not a comprehensive glossary of the Internet
or of the information industry; there are many excellent glossaries
and reference sources for basic terminology, and it is not my inten-
tion to attempt to replicate those here.

What I found most exciting about my interviews with these Super
Searchers was their enthusiasm about the future of information
resources and of information experts. Our skills in evaluating, analyzing, synthesizing and managing information are becoming more

valued every day. The Internet and the resulting complaints of information overload and data smog are the equivalent of the Information Professionals' Full Employment Act of 2000, as people struggle to keep up with a changing information landscape. Our career paths may mutate and take unexpected changes, but they sure won't be boring.

# Jan Tudor
## Business Valuation Research

Jan Tudor is an independent research
librarian and the owner of JT Research,
based in Portland, OR.

JanTudor@JTResearch.com
www.JTResearch.com

## Tell me a bit about your background and how you wound up where you are today.

I've always been kind of a research nerd. I was one of those people in college who loved term papers. I worked in a law library before going on to grad school to get my M.L.I.S. at the University of California, Berkeley, and when I got out of library school, my first professional job was at Willamette University in Salem, Oregon. I was a basic reference librarian there for a few years, and then I branched out and became their business librarian. I became very frustrated in the academic environment, so I moved on to the corporate world and landed an awesome job at Willamette Management Associates.

After I was there for a couple of years, I became frustrated with the eight-to-five environment and with having so many ideas but not being able to carry them out. In particular, I wanted to be highly involved in the marketing of the company. Willamette Management is one of the leading business valuation firms in the country, and I saw how, in my position as director of the library, I could really branch out and help the analysts and owners with their marketing efforts. The problem was that I had to do so much research and couldn't hire more people, so I just couldn't grow. I wanted to do so much more and I couldn't. So in May 1997, I decided to move on and start my own business.

My time at Willamette Management was really useful for me. As the head of research for a firm that is so well known in the industry, I had other appraisers calling me all the time, asking me how to do research or how to find a certain piece of information. The more I learned about the industry, the more I realized there was this whole niche market out there of people who couldn't afford librarians and who didn't have time to do the research themselves. So while I was at Willamette, I started thinking, "Gee, I've identified this market. I'm just going to shoot for that." And I did. I started saving business cards, did a lot of public speaking to appraisers, saved every conference attendee list that I could, and that's how I started. And it's where I am today.

## What kind of research do you do now, and what kinds of clients do you have?

I'd say ninety percent of my clients are business appraisers. A business appraiser will get hired by the owner of a privately held company for a couple of reasons. One reason would be that the owner wants to sell the company. Another reason would be that it's the end of the year, and the business owner wants to give some shares to a family member. Or maybe there's a divorce going on and the company needs to be valued for the property settlement, but because the company doesn't have stock on the public market, it's hard to come up with a value. So there's this whole set of rules that business appraisers use to come up with a company's value. They have to look at how the company compares to the rest of its industry. And oddly enough, there is an Internal Revenue Code ruling that mandates that you must do this research, which is great for me. That's only for gift tax valuations, but it sets the tone for the whole industry.

So when the appraisers go through their checklist of rules for valuing a company, they need to conduct research, and they don't know how to do it. Mind you, the research isn't a big part of the valuation—it's more like due diligence for them—but there are times when my research carries a lot of weight, such as when it's for litigation.

What it comes down to is that I do a lot of industry research; every day, I get a different industry. Yesterday I did swimming pool contractors; the day before, I did plastic injection molding. Every day, it's something new and, geek that I am, I love it. I also do a lot of company research using public company data, finding comparable mergers for a proposed acquisition for comparison purposes. And every once in a while I get a business broker who wants industry research.

## I remember hearing you speak at the Online World conference, and you mentioned that research is like making a cocktail. Can you explain that?

It really *does* describe my standard research methodology. It's what enables me to manage my time and manage the tremendous number of data sources we have now. I really had to come up with this to save my soul, my mental health. So here's how it works. I get the call from a client: "All right, I'm going to value a plastic injection molding company," and I have the typical reference interview with the person. I'll ask, "Who are their customers, what geographic area does this company work in, do they export?" I try to get as much information as I can so that I can understand exactly what the client needs. That's what makes my job a bit easier. I even write up this discussion and include it in the final report.

Once I get ready to actually begin the research, I pull out the *Encyclopedia of Business Information Sources* [79, see Appendix A]. This is the ironic thing—I start my online research with a book! And I pull out Trip Wyckoff's *SI: Special Issues* [95], and I check *Fulltext Sources Online* [83], just to get a feel of where the industry is. The *Encyclopedia of Business Information Sources* is amazing—it saves me so much time. It helps me identify the trade associations, the major newsletters and the trade publications, and if there are any relevant research institutes. I find this technique really valuable because I'm outsourcing more, and I'm outsourcing to people who aren't librarians. They're learning how to search and I want to give them some guidelines. So I make this checklist as a starting point— these are the trade associations to call, and so on. When I worked at Willamette University, I taught a lot of library instruction classes, and I always said to the students, "It's so important to start with a reference book, because it gets you grounded; you can jump off from there." I'm finally practicing what I preach.

Once I get an idea of some of the major publications and the trade associations in the industry I'm researching, then I go online. For example, if I have identified an industry's trade association, I will go directly to the Internet, either to the ASAE [4] site or I'll do a phrase search with that association's name in one or two search engines to locate its Web site. I'll check out the association's site to see how much information they're providing. Sometimes, they'll just give you a little bit and sometimes they'll give you a ton of information. If the Web site doesn't have a lot of information, then I will go to the Industry Insider product on Investext [37] and see if the industry is covered there. And if the Web site mentions any association publications, I might look in *Fulltext Sources Online* to see if the publications are available online. Of course, not everything is online. I like Trip Wyckoff's *Special Issues* because he covers a lot of publications that aren't online, and there might be an amazing industry overview in a publication that has just never made it online. But I feel like I've covered all my bases with those three print sources.

So to get back to my analogy of my research 'cocktail,' this is sort of like my liquor cabinet. My reference resources are my liquor cabinet, where I look to see what I want to do. So I decide to start with the rum—this is the trade association information and whatever I can find on Investext. And I might make some phone calls.

For example, *Special Issues* might tell me that the December issue of a journal has a forecast of the industry I'm researching, so I might fax a note to the editor and ask that it be sent to me. The next thing I know, I have the whole issue sitting here in my fax machine. It's something I do as part of my routine, just to see if I can get a jump on things, before trying to find it online.

And then I'm going to add my Kahlua to my rum drink. That's when I go to Dialog [20]. I will go to the typical files—9, 15, 16, 148 and 636—*[Editor's note: Business & Industry, ABI/Inform, IAC PROMT, IAC Business & Industry Database, and IAC Newsletter Database]* to find industry information. I know the indexing really well in those files, and I'll look for index terms such as "industry-wide conditions" or "forecasts." I will do some quick searching, print out the results in format 8, which shows index terms, or sometimes format 6 even though it frustrates me because the title doesn't necessarily indicate what the article's about. Then I'll look the results over and I'll think, "Okay, here are a couple of really good articles; I'd rather just buy them online than spend more time trying to find them cheaper anywhere else." And I read through the articles I've just downloaded.

Now we come to my next ingredient, which is Triple Sec, an orange liqueur. That's when I go back to the Internet, because I might read in one of the articles I downloaded that there's a trade association I've missed, or there's a consulting firm that covers the industry, or somebody's name shows up as an expert. I kind of play with it; I go back and forth between the for-fee online services and the Internet. That's where my creative bartending skills come into play.

Next I add the coffee—information that is on the Internet that is not available on a fee-based online service. Maybe I can find research that a student or a professor did. I will also go to what I consider my "known" sites like the Census Bureau [14] and consulting firms such as CIT [16], which publishes industry overviews on the Net that never appear in the traditional online services. I rely heavily on my bookmark files; it isn't until I'm really desperate that I will use a search engine.

I'm lucky that I have a formula that works for me and that I get to do the same type of research every day, because it's allowed me to create a rhythm in my searching—or my bartending. And finally, if I still need some more information, I'll add my final ingredient. This is the cream that goes on top of this drink—what I've described is called a Spanish Coffee. I will go to a market research database. Typically, I go to Dialog, because it's so time-consuming to go to each consulting firm's Web site and find the tables of contents. I'm kind of wishy-washy about that, though; it all depends on how much time and money I've spent already. With Dialog's DialUnit pricing, doing research on the market research files in Dialog is so expensive now. It just boggles my mind that I can come up with a $30 Dialog bill, and all I did was get tables of contents from market research reports.

When I pay that much for what was essentially just the catalog of reports, I realize that I need to make a bookmark file of all the market research sites on the Net, and just make that part of my routine. What I really like about some of those consulting firms' sites is that they put out press releases. Sometimes that will give me the one sentence that I need. Another fee-based service I'll use at the very end if I haven't found anything else is Investext's investment banking reports.

So that's my recipe for industry research and for a Spanish Coffee. When the drink is served, they light the rum on fire and it's quite spectacular. That's how I feel when I deliver the research project to the client—ta-da! I know I've done the best I can, given the budget that I have. The client wanted the current status of the industry and forecasts of where it is heading, and when I finally am done with my research and it leaves my office with my name on it, I know I'm delivering a good product.

# It sounds like you have integrated the Net into your research; obviously, there's a lot that you can do now on the Net that you couldn't do a few years ago. How do you think your searching has changed because of the Net?

It goes back to this recipe I use for searching. My searching of the professional online services is pretty systematic, and I guess I'm a bit impatient when it comes to the Net. I don't have a lot of time and patience to sit back and marvel at the glory of the Internet and say, "Isn't all of this just incredibly wonderful? And I love these images! And look at that Java applet!" I don't care about all that. On the other hand, I don't feel that I've done a good search unless I've searched the Internet. It goes back to my offering due diligence research for my clients—I could miss something really important if I don't look on the Internet.

I don't know if the Net has changed my searching, but it's added a different component to it. There is definitely some juggling of time and budget that I had to figure out. Let me explain first how I price my services for my clients: I decided to make it sort of a package, you get an industry researched for X dollars. At first, I thought I could save my clients a lot of money by going to the library, because the public libraries here in Portland are amazing. But that required me to walk down to the library and I realized that, although I was saving my clients some money in online costs, it was taking me twice as long to do the work. So over a period of about a year I fine-tuned how much time I was willing to spend online and how much money I could justify charging the client, because the cost of my product is what the market will bear.

The other thing about search habits is that it's so important to know the search engines, yet it's hard to break my old habits and get proficient on the new Net search tools. I guess that goes back to my lack of patience and why I love Dialog—I know how to search it and it stays reasonably stable. With all the new search engines coming out, I feel like I'm starting from square one all the time. While at a conference, I heard people saying, "Hey, did you hear about Northern Light?" And I thought, "What?" I feel like I just keep getting farther behind. But that's why those conferences are important; they help me keep up on new developments that I might not discover on my own.

## Do you get many clients saying, "Gosh, you used the Internet for this; why are you charging me so much money?"

Nope. If they did, I'd say, "OK, go do it yourself." A lot of my clients come to me because they've found out that research isn't all that easy on the Net, and they don't have the time to figure it out anyway. Sometimes I'll get a client who will tell me that they have someone in-house who's looked all over the Internet and that they realize they need to hire me, because what they needed wasn't on the Internet after all.

I pay for a table-top exhibit at about three trade shows a year. The Internet's always the hook, and I even give out a bibliography of my favorite Internet sites for business appraisers. I know that even if they used all of the links I provided, chances are they won't find enough to write an overview. And they'll say, "Gosh what a great job you have! You do all your work on the Internet." And I say, "No, I only do about thirty percent of my research on the Net."

## There are so many databases available in a number of formats and on a number of online services. How do you decide which format and which source to use?

A lot depends on the interface. Take Investext as an example. I've looked at it on Dow Jones [21], I've looked at it on Dialog,

I've looked at it on Investext's I/Plus Direct, and I truly like it best on Dialog.

It's the same with market research reports. I might pay a little more on Dialog, but I don't care because I don't have to learn a new search language or figure out a new interface. In general, I won't log on to the Internet just to save a dollar. I get dumped off the Net at least three times a day, and I'd rather pay a premium to know that's not going to happen during a search. As a matter of fact, that's what bothers me about Dow Jones moving to the Web, although I understand that they're still supporting dial-up access. I love dial-up, and I just think it's a much better connection. So whether or not I have to access a service through the Net is one of the biggest factors in deciding where I'm going to search a particular database.

The same goes for selecting one online service over another if it'll save me a dollar here or there. If I'm taking an extra half-hour to do a search on a service I'm not as familiar with, that's a big chunk of my profit. When I set the price for my average industry profile, I allot myself three hours for research. If I take an extra half-hour to find the information, I'm eating away at my profits.

It's especially tricky since I'm outsourcing more. I don't have the time to teach that person how to search Dialog. I know the new version of DialogWeb will alleviate some of my worries. But that just complicates the decision of which service to recommend. Which one do I tell her to use? Which one do I train her on?

## How do you stay updated on all the new search engines and online services that are coming out?

I probably don't do it very well. For search engines, I rely on Greg Notess [91], and I always read his columns. And I read *Searcher* [94], *Database* [77] and *Online* [92] cover to cover. I love *CyberSkeptic's Guide* [76]; it looks more to the practical side of searching. I also read *Yahoo! Internet Life* [101], and any of the other Internet magazines when I see them. I'm out of control—I even read when I work out on the Stairmaster. Some people are reading *People* magazine, and I'm reading *Internet Life*.

## Do you rely much on electronic discussion groups?

No, they bother me. It's just that I suffer from information overload. I've sometimes seen things that I've wanted to respond to, but I don't get around to it until it's way too late. I do like the SLA Business & Finance listserv [67], because when someone posts something there, I know it's a good question.

## What do you do when you are in the middle of a search and just not finding what you want?

When I am flailing, I will usually pick up the phone and call people in a relevant trade association. I'll say "I have done all of this and this and this, and I'm still having trouble finding information." People are usually pretty kind; they'll say, "Well, when you find it, let me know." *They* don't know! And that's confirmation for me that I'm not really out to lunch. If this head person in an industry group says "Good luck!" maybe the information just isn't out there. Sometimes I'll call an expert researcher in the field and ask, "Am I missing something here, or is this just a really hard search?"

## Have you noticed an impact of electronic mail on your business clients? Are they expecting reports to be delivered sooner or in electronic format?

A lot of people want things in email. And the issue of immediacy is a real problem. A lot of my clients call me because they've waited until the last minute, or they've tried to do the research themselves and now they're up against a wall. Unfortunately for me, they also need hard copies for their files. I have yet to have a client tell me to just put it on a diskette and mail it to him. For that matter, I'm still going to the library and photocopying material for clients. So I email what I can, but I always follow up with hard copy. I'm certainly not a paperless office.

## How do you handle delivering information from Web sites? Do you print it off and send it to your clients, or do you give them the URL so they can go get it themselves?

My whole thing is service, so I'll print it out. My clients are hiring me to save them from all of that. But I should mention that the Internet poses special problems for me. I do a lot of historical research, because a business valuation means that the business is going to be valued at a specific point in time. The rule of thumb is that all the information you find must have been available before that specific point in time. Say the valuation date is December 31, 1998. I cannot use anything published after that date. This is where the Internet has posed some problems for me; I might find something outrageously great on the Internet but there's no date on it, so I have to email the Webmaster and ask when this page was published. If the valuation ever went to court and they found out that they were using data published after the valuation date, they could get in big trouble.

I treat what I am looking at on the Internet as if it were in a hard-copy magazine. I'm always looking for a publication date. I'm just afraid that it will say, "This was added to the Internet on XYZ date," which doesn't mean anything to me. I'm still not assured that the information was actually available on the valuation date. If it's not perfectly clear to me, I will write to the person managing the Web site and save their reply. It's just due diligence; I have to do it to cover myself. Some appraisers don't care, but as far as I'm concerned, it's pretty important.

I deal with a lot of issues involving reliability and retrievability of Net sites. In fact, I'm calling someone at a trade association today about a great chart that's on their site. It talks about yearly sales of swimming pools, but it doesn't indicate whether the figures are in millions or thousands, and there is no date on the Web site so I can't tell how current it is. Fortunately, I've had pretty good luck in getting people to respond to me. In fact, after I gave a presentation at the Online World conference, someone from the National Restaurant Association came up to me and said "I know you! You've called us several times, and I recognize your name."

## Maybe if enough of us keep asking those questions, they'll do a better job of self-documenting the Web sites. Can you describe a project that was particularly interesting or fun?

It was when I was working with Kevin Kelly as he was writing his book, *New Rules for the New Economy*. What made this job interesting, fun and challenging was that he is such a thinker. I hate to use this cliché, but he really does push the envelope, and he made me do that too. Once I got started, I realized that if I was going to do the type of job he wanted me to do, I would have to extend my thinking. What was so fun was that it made me fall back on a lot of theory that I learned in library school—like the old question, "Who would publish this? Who would care?"

It took research to a whole different level for me. I was out calling people. I was physically out of my office doing primary research. I really had to span the disciplines, and that's what I remember most about library school—being challenged to think outside of your typical research patterns. Instead of just thinking,

"What database do I use?" I was looking at historical material in the library, I was online, I was all over the place. It was a great project, because it did challenge my whole notion about how to find information. I did a lot of Internet research, but it was really tough work.

For example, he asked me a question about what the world is worth: What is it worth to replace all the infrastructure in the world? I worked on that for hours. I thought that maybe the insurance industry could help me because everything's insured, right? Maybe I could at least come up with a base that you could make a model on. I was really pushing it, and a lot of times I just came up with zero. It was both a dream project and a nightmare project, because it was so challenging and I really felt like I was being pushed to the maximum. I never met Kevin face to face, but he sent me a copy of the book when it finally came out with the nicest note in it. He said that this book couldn't have been what it was without my help, and that my research allowed him to go much deeper than he could have otherwise.

## What do you enjoy most about this profession? What keeps you doing this instead of going out and being a gardener or something?

I think a lot of it is my personality; I like finding the answer, knowing it's out there. And I like being able to use my brain to figure out a question and to answer it. The more years I have in the profession and the better I get at it, the more satisfying it is. I'm rarely bored. Maybe the searching is routine, but I always learn something. And I find that extremely rewarding.

## And what do you like least about it?

When my computer crashes or when I get bounced off the Web. The technology just gets in the way of finding the information. One thing that I really liked about Kevin Kelly's project was that I got to go to the library and sit there with stacks of books. My next career will be as a massage therapist or working with search and rescue dogs, I swear. Not that I'm a Luddite, but sometimes it seems that there's just too much of a focus on the technology.

## What are your thoughts about the future of the information professional?

I don't know if our jobs will change that much in the next five years or so. I think there may be more demand for our services, because people only have so much time in the day to find information. I think that our role will always involve looking over information and synthesizing it for people, acting as a filter. That's where I think we're very important. Sure, you can get thirty articles on a subject, but does someone really want to read thirty articles? I think we will definitely need more subject expertise. There's so much information out there; we should be the ones who have the knowledge to say, "Don't look at that—that's not viable information; look here instead."

I really hope that we don't lose the ability to do command-language online searching. All these vendors trying to attract the end-user market makes me fear that the information product itself is going to suffer. At a conference, I heard a public records researcher say, "Don't forget about all the value-added features of a fee-based service." It's so easy to look at conference exhibits and think, "Wow! This is only going to cost me a dollar!" or, "You can get it on the Web so much cheaper." But you might lose a lot of the indexing, or you might lose a lot of other qualities of the databases that we like so much. The public records speaker said, "Don't get caught up in all of the fervor of 'get it on the Web,'" and I completely agree with that. For all the glitz of the Net, there are still reasons to use the tried-and-true services. We can do more powerful searching, we have a lot more control over the searching, and we understand what the universe is that we're searching. All of that makes for a better information product at the end.

I remember Patrick Wilson, one of my professors in library school, who gave these crazy lectures. He'd stand on the edge of the platform, and he'd be preaching, practically. "Don't forget the big picture, and don't forget who would write about it. Who cares about this information?" I think about that all the time. If I walked away with one thing from library school, it was what he said. When I get really carried away on the Web, when I'm following links and I can't find something, I log off and I think back to that. And I realize that it might not even be online—what a concept! That became perfectly clear with Kevin Kelly's project.

# Super Searcher Power Tips:

► I've developed a standard research methodology. It's what enables me to manage my time and manage the tremendous number of data sources we have now. I had to come up with a routine to save my mental health.

► This is the ironic thing—I start my online research with a book! Once I get an idea of some of the major publications and the trade associations in the industry I'm researching, then I go online.

► When I search Dialog, I'll look for index terms such as "industry-wide conditions" or "forecasts."

► I rely heavily on my bookmark files; it isn't until I'm really desperate that I will use a Web search engine.

► I think that our role will always involve looking over information and synthesizing it for people, acting as a filter. That's where I think we're very important.

# Seymour Satin
## One-Man Library

Seymour Satin is the manager of library/information services at Atlantic Richfield Co. in Los Angeles. He has worked in the information industry for more than 25 years.

ssatin@mail.arco.com

## Can you tell me a little bit about your background? What brought you to ARCO?

I started off at a branch library of the Los Angeles Public Library as a messenger clerk, and I loved it. I was there for almost three years. Then I moved over to the central library; I was there in the general reader services department for three and a half years. One of the department's clients was ARCO, and they kept telling me they had an opening. I finally went for an interview and they offered me a position as a photocopy clerk. It meant I would lose the research work I'd been doing, but honestly, the money was almost double what I was earning at the central library, so I took the job.

I worked my way up from there. I saw people searching, and I just stayed after work observing them—I thought this was the greatest thing I'd ever seen. I had to stay after work since I couldn't watch them during the day, because it wasn't part of my job description. They noticed my interest; I guess I was asking some good questions. So they put me in bibliographic verification, which was part of the document delivery service we offered, and we all discovered that I had a knack for searching—and I loved it. They started reducing staff in 1985 from eleven people to five, and I moved into the

17

information specialist position, and then senior information specialist. In 1995 we cut down from five to two, and when somebody left in October of that year, I became the sole person.

## How would you describe a typical ARCO library client?

That's hard to say, since things have changed so much. My typical day a year ago is not my typical day now—and that's what I love about it. Even though I've been in the same library since 1980, it changes constantly. There are three major libraries within ARCO— the one in Plano, Texas, which is basically a technical library that handles patents, scientific, engineering, geophysics and petroleum-related questions; the library in Anchorage, Alaska, which is split fifty-fifty between technical and business-type questions; and my library, which is ninety-five percent business and five percent technical. So, even though I'm in a petroleum company, the library I work in is a business library.

I do a lot of work finding competitive intelligence, background on mergers and acquisitions, marketing information, that sort of thing. I do get into specific oil questions like crude prices and share of market, but basically it's a business library. We find information on doing business in other countries—everything from politics to the economy to social issues for expatriates. My major clients are the planning groups in the operating companies, then the treasurer's office, the control and audit groups, and the products and marketing people.

## When you get a research request, how do you decide where to begin?

I can't say I go on the Net first; I can't say I go on Dialog or to a print source. It really depends on the question. I really don't have anything set because each question is different and it's always possible that the patron has already done some initial work. Everyone has

Internet access at the desktop, so one of the first questions—after finding out what they're looking for—is what have they done already, so I don't duplicate their work. If they have done some initial research, I might ask them, "Well, how did you search it?" just to see if they've even done it correctly.

## Obviously, the scope and depth of information that's on the Net has grown exponentially over the last few years. How has that changed how you do research?

I think the Net has definitely helped us, but it has also hurt us in our professional standing with our clients because a lot of people think, "Oh, I have the Net, I've got everything, I don't need the library's services." Part of our job is to educate the client about what the Net has and what it doesn't have. That has to be an ongoing process, especially with the new breed of people coming in—the new MBAs and so on—who think that the Net has everything. We need to keep educating them on information gathering and data integrity. If they say they've gone on the Net and I know what project they're working on, and a major business decision is being based on information gathered from the Web, I get worried. A lot of sites aren't even documented, so they couldn't even tell me where they got the information, except to say, "I got it off the Net." That should concern all of us in the information service industry, because it could be some guy from a garage sending out data. If the information is going to be used for an important business decision, it has to come from a reliable source. That's one thing I preach.

Some of the questions that come in are from people asking me to verify something they found on the Net with a second source. I'm always glad to see that. I also spend time educating people about the fact that a lot of the really good hard-core data is never going to be free on the Net. I remind my clients that nobody's going to give away information if they can make money on it.

I have to say that my searching of professional online services has gone down, because some of the simpler questions are handled by the Net—from addresses to basic things like information on outsourcing. The Outsourcing Institute [49, see Appendix A] has a lot up on their Web site—articles, special reports and material that you can purchase from them. That has really helped us quite a bit. But I do advocate using the pay-per-view systems.

## When you're doing a search on the Net, do you start with one of your bookmarked sites or do you use one of the broad search engines?

It really depends on the question. I have a very large bookmark file, and a lot of my searches are repetitive—a company profile, or information from a government agency. I have my usual sources bookmarked so I can go right to them, which saves time. Unfortunately, my bookmark file isn't too well-organized. I have categories, but I keep adding more bookmarks. I probably have fifty to insert into categories right now. If I can't find what I'm looking for in my bookmark file quickly, then I definitely do a Net search. But I try to go right to the source first instead of spending time on a search engine.

## What professional online services do you use the most?

Lexis-Nexis [40] is a primary source, along with Dialog [20] and Dow Jones [21]. We also have a number of industry-specific enterprise-wide contracts. One of the things I love is negotiating contracts for the corporation's offices around the world. I identify what we subscribe to across the board, then I consolidate the subscriptions enterprise wide and put the material out on our corporate intranet.

## How do you handle the pricing for enterprise-wide contracts? Is it part of the library's budget or do you bill that back?

Right now, we're pondering that question and the whole process of how to charge back the enterprise-wide services. Some of the methods being considered involve dividing the costs among the operating companies based on the number of employees, and charging back based on actual usage. Since we just started the consolidation of information services into enterprise-wide contracts, I have started to budget for these items in the library budget.

## How do you decide which sources to put up on the intranet?

You have to know what the needs are in your company. In our industry, we have the *John S. Harold Oil Headliner* and we have *Platt's Oilgram News*, and both of those are available to everyone at ARCO on a daily basis via the Net. There are so many good services out there; at the same time, you don't want to put your clients on "information overload." My two major factors in determining what we put out on the intranet are ease of use and the timeliness of the information, which is very important.

## If you know that the same information is available for free on the Net and also available on one of the for-fee online services, how do you decide which source to use?

To me, it's a question of the cost of going online versus me sitting there waiting for the browser to pull up my document and then going from page to page. Often my clients need the information right away—they're in a meeting and need it fast—so I definitely go on a for-fee system just so I can get the information to the client right away.

## How do you stay updated on new services, new features, new search engines, and on the information industry as a whole?

Basically I network, because for me networking is the best source. When I see something interesting, I will call a few people, and I get calls from others asking, "Did you see ...?" or "Did you hear ...?" A lot of times, you'll hear gossip about a new product or service. A vendor might tell one client, "This is coming out soon and you're the first one to know." Trust me, that gets passed along to the librarian network immediately. I also rely on library listservs to keep me updated; I subscribe to SLA's Business & Finance Division listserv [67] and the Information Technology Division listserv [70]. I also go to professional conferences, where I pick up a lot of information; I belong to SLA [99], SCOUG [98], SCALL [97], and SCIP [96]. The three primary print sources that I use to keep updated are *Information Today* [88], *Searcher* [94], and *Database* [77] magazines. They keep you up to date on where things are going and what's new. But I still rely heavily on my network.

## How do you know when you're finished with a search? Do you base it on a not-to-exceed budget? Do you just know when you've found all you're going to find?

First, I have to emphasize that we do not base our searches on a not-to-exceed budget. I answer the question, no matter what it takes. To me, the most important part of the search process is the interview with the client. I will not let my client go until I fully understand what's needed. You also have to build a rapport with your clients, so you understand their wants, needs and expectations.

To answer your question about when I know I'm finished with a search, well, sometimes you're never done. You have to understand the question and give the client the best answer you can. You also have to work with the client if you can't fully understand what their need is; have them sit with you during your online search and follow up afterward to see if what you produced was useful. I refuse to give somebody an inch-high pile of paper to wade through. If that ever happened, I'd know that I didn't do my job correctly.

And when someone says, "I want everything on ..." I normally won't accept that as a research question. There have to be some parameters, even if it's just limiting by date or limiting the research to certain publications. Of course, I've had the opposite problem too—someone asks for a single article and I can't find it anywhere. After I've done all the searching I can do, I'll kick it back to the client and say, "Are you sure it's from the *Los Angeles Times* on this date? Where did you see the article, or how did you hear about it?" I'll put the question back to the client to verify the source or give me more information. I don't do overkill; I don't spend extra money when it's not appropriate. Having done this for so many years, you just know when enough is enough.

## Do you find that you're doing more of that information filtering than you used to? Do you think that clients tolerate fewer "data dumps" than in the past?

Yes, although "filtering" to me is a dangerous word. As long as I've understood their question and I can give them some information that answers their question, or if I see something that might be related to it, I'll do the filtering of the search results. But I don't want to suggest that I do very much synthesis of the results. I think it's important to give the client a good variety of information sources. As I said before, it's a matter of understanding their questions, and most questions call for more than just a yes or no answer or, "You want-ed this, here it is."

Sometimes clients will say, "I really don't know what I want, so I want to see everything, and that will help me focus on what I'm looking for." My response to them is, "OK, close your eyes. I've already finished the search and you have the perfect article in your hand. What's the title of that article?" And I really have them close their eyes! Based on their response, sometimes I've thrown away my interview notes and I've started all over again, because what they told me prior to that did not even come close to the title they just gave me.

**One of the big services that librarians provide during the reference interview is helping the client figure out what it is they need. They often don't know what their question is until they've talked to a librarian about it. One of our skills is helping them articulate their information needs.**

It's a hard skill to develop, but to be successful in our industry, you have to know how to interview. You could have all the online skills in the world, but that doesn't help if you don't understand the question and you can't really give the client what they need. I've had a lot of searchers working for me over the years. Some of them were great searchers, but some insisted on giving the client piles of paper because they really didn't have a good understanding of the question. I don't believe in making the client go through a wad of paper checking off what he or she wants. Let's give the clients exactly what they need so they can do their jobs. That's why I feel I've been successful here at ARCO—besides my charm.

# How do you handle a research project where you understand the question but you have no idea where to start?

I take a step back and I break down the question. Sometimes I'll walk through my print reference section, just glancing at it. I know my collection pretty well, but sometimes I'll forget about that one little book, and I'll stumble on it and think, "I haven't used that in a while, hmmm, I wonder" and—boom—there's the answer. After that, I'll quickly flip through the online search guides for Lexis or Dialog, to see what files might pertain to the question. A lot of times I use the network within my corporation. Someone from one group might have already done something like this or at least have some suggestions. My secret here is to network and never take "no" for an answer. If the person I'm talking to says "No, I don't have a clue," then my next question would be, "Who do you know that would?" Never give up!

# How you handle the opposite problem, when you have a really broad research topic and you're having trouble narrowing it down?

Again, that goes back to the interview and the expectations of the client. I ask questions like, "What kind of publications are you looking for? Are you looking for technical material or general publications?" That helps you select your databases. If someone wants something very general, you just search general magazines. If someone wants more theoretical material, then you might try an ABI/Inform search. If they want conference proceedings, that tells you where you're going to go. So it's part of the reference interview: "What exactly are you looking for, and what are you going to do with this data when I get it for you?"

If a client tells me they want everything on a company, my response is, "Well, do you mean press releases, general magazine articles, case studies?" Part of the interview process leads you to the databases. You could spend a lot of money playing around online, trying to get an idea of where to go, when your clients already have an idea of what they want. You just have to get it out of them.

I've learned that it helps if you can make them more relaxed. I have candy at my desk, and I joke around with clients a bit. Instead of clients coming in to my office all stressed-out and saying, "I need this and I need it now," I try to make them feel relaxed so they'll be able to speak more freely. Sometimes, they'll admit that the question is really for their boss and they don't know exactly what to look for. Then I can tell them to either have the boss call me or let me call the boss. When you play "telephone searching," so to speak, you're just not going to do a successful search. I always go right to the source; it doesn't matter how high up it is. I have a very hard time doing a search if it's filtered through a secretary or an intern, since they'll usually just repeat the request without a good understanding of what their boss really needs. They're not going to get good results, and that could lead to a waste of time and money.

## Do you hear many questions from clients asking you why you can't just get everything you need from the Net?

Unfortunately, that has been the mystique with the Net. I do hear, "You know, your services aren't all that necessary because it's all on the Net." I remind them that the Net is great but you get what you pay for, and that only very generic items are on the Net. You find some information there, but the really good material is going to be on the pay services. I have to market that idea a bit more. When I have an online end-user training class come in, one thing I always remind them is that there are other systems out there besides the Net. No one service can answer every question. Sometimes you have to go to a number of different resources to get a complete answer. So don't ever rely on just one system, be it the Net or Lexis-Nexis, Dialog or Dow Jones.

## How do you deliver material to clients? Are you sending most of your search results electronically, or do they still prefer hard copy?

I do a lot of emailing. I'll try to download my search results in a nice, clean format so that it doesn't require much cleaning up. I'll throw the results into a Word document and then send it out. I use hard-copy sources too, so then I use interoffice mail or I fax it. We're on Lotus Notes, so it's pretty easy to send attachments throughout the corporation. When I need to send something from the Net, I just include the hot link through Notes, and all they have to do is click on it and read or print it out. That way, I don't have to spend time downloading and formatting the material from the Web. I am happy to say that, over the years, ARCO personnel have become accustomed to electronic information, and that is the preferred method of delivery.

## Can you describe a recent research project that you found particularly challenging or fun?

You know, it could be the simplest thing. Sometimes it's tracking down a single article; the client is probably wrong about the date or the publication, or no one has that journal in their collection, but when you finally track it down anyway, well, that's pretty satisfying. I find it very rewarding to know that I'm part of a large decision-making process—that others use my data in their decision making. It doesn't really matter if I get credit or not. Sometimes I might hear a remark on the elevator or on the floor: "Hey, you gave us some good stuff there; we found it really useful." That is the really satisfying part of my job. There have been major deals–litigation matters, or when ARCO spun off a division, or possible acquisition deals—

and I was on call whenever they needed something, even late at night or early in the morning. That makes me feel good.

## That's definitely the satisfying part of this profession. What do you find most frustrating about this kind of work?

There have been situations where an online vendor will represent that they have everything on their service, and it takes a lot of work and analysis on our part to figure out what they really offer. You have to do your homework and compare sources and services to identify the best product available to meet your needs. Sometimes my clients will tell me, "This vendor contacted me directly and said they have everything we need, so let's sign up and get the system now." It makes my job more difficult, having to explain how the vendor may have misled the client into believing that their product had more to offer than it really does.

It's important to keep up with professional reading and with list-servs; you learn what's going on and who offers what. These days, I keep hearing the major vendors saying the same thing: "We can meet all your business needs in our system." And I know that's not true. This is the most frustrating thing to me professionally.

## Where do you think the information profession is heading? Will we still be doing much research? Will we still be intermediaries?

I remember doing a presentation with a Predicasts sales rep back in 1987 at the Online World conference, and speculating that our roles were going to change, that we would be information consultants teaching our clients how to use all the end-user systems that were coming. I still believe that is where we're headed. I definitely took that role here at ARCO, as an educator and guide showing clients how to use the information services that are available to them. I still do searching, but I also stay in close contact with my clients, understanding and anticipating their information needs. My recommendation is to get a good grasp on what information services and experts currently exist in your company. This gets you into knowledge management – I know that's considered a buzzword nowadays, but the bottom line is that it allows you to share information, reduce costs and work more efficiently. The other role I see for us is organizing and negotiating enterprise-wide information contracts. This takes a lot of work, but who is better qualified to do this than the company librarian?

# Super Searcher Power Tips

► Part of our job is to educate the client about what the Net has and what it doesn't have, about information gathering and data integrity. That has to be an ongoing process, especially with the new breed of people coming in, who think that the Net has everything.

► Remember your internal resources and network—you might not have to go onto the professional online services to answer your question.

► The most important part of research is the interview process. The interview process leads you to the resources, which lead you to the answer.

# Linda Cooper

## Independent Info Pro and End User

Linda Cooper is an independent information professional based in Quakertown, PA, and the editor of BiblioData's *Price Watcher*. She was profiled in *Secrets of the Super Searchers*.

LindaCooper@erols.com

## First, why don't you go into a little bit of your background and how you got to where you are today?

I went to Temple University in Philadelphia to study painting, because I didn't want to do anything academic. But when I graduated with my painting degree, I realized I was going to have a pretty hard time earning a living. I took a job in the advertising department of a local department store as a runner and enjoyed it very much, but realized that I wasn't going to get very far. So I called Drexel University about librarianship because my mother was a teacher and, since I didn't want to be a teacher, librarianship sounded second best. My first job after I graduated from Drexel was at the Institute for Scientific Information, where I built its first corporate library and did research for Dr. Eugene Garfield. I developed a really excellent working relationship with him, and since he was an entrepreneur, he encouraged me to be an entrepreneur myself. In fact, he told me something along the lines of "If you can please me with my research needs, you can probably succeed as an information broker."

31

In 1982, information brokering was really new and not well defined. I knew a lot about back-of-the-book indexing, because one of the things that I had done at ISI was index Gene Garfield's essays in *Information Scientist*. So I contacted the University of Pennsylvania and Princeton and some other university presses and started indexing books. I did a lot of freelance work for the Institute in my first couple of years as an independent. Gradually, I started poking around in new areas of information brokering and I began doing online searches for a fee, which was considered pretty "out there" at the time.

After my first year, I got a business partner, Pat Heller. We used to make this joke all the time—everything was so new, and we were scrambling to learn how to do what we were trying to do and how to explain it to people—so we said that if people called us and said, "We need a search on the market for tea in China, and we need our drive-way paved," we would say yes to both.

Anyway, we built the company and eventually sold it to a large information provider, Teltech, in 1995. I worked for Teltech for three years as part of the agreement of sale, and then I went out on my own again as an independent. So, counting when I worked at the Temple University library while I was in library school, my sequence of jobs has been in academic, corporate, independent, corporate, and independent settings.

## How would you describe what you do now?

I do three kinds of things. I do online research for clients, most of whom actually are other independent information professionals who need to bring in a good business searcher for this or that. I do project management for corporate librarians who simply have too much on their desks and need someone to make sure things are moving along. These are usually managerial projects, as in rewriting process stan-dards or best practices—and I can do that because of the number of years that I've had in the field. And third, I do some editing and writing of newsletters, articles and speeches.

## I guess writing articles and speeches requires some of the same kind of research that you do for clients.

Exactly. I am my own end user. We information professionals teach our constituents to become end users to the extent they are comfortable with it. They will turn to us for projects that are clearly beyond their ability or time frame, and then, because the bar has been raised about the quality of research and the type of research that we supply them, we have to do our own end-user searching. We then synthesize the information, analyze it and write up a report for them—our constituents never really see the searching that was done. This is very different from 1977 when I started my career. Back then, clients got a search summary in a paragraph, if they were lucky. Now they get full-blown reports, spreadsheets, charts, graphs, diagrams, PowerPoint presentations, and so forth. So when I'm doing my searching I'm really doing it for myself, because the deliverable is no longer the search output, but an analysis of the search results.

## That's an interesting way of describing it— that we do our own end-user searching now. That means we all need to think about whether we are information retrievers or information analysts.

That's right. It's sort of a Darwinian thing. We are evolving up the food chain, definitely. And part of the reason is that technology is catching up with where we were ten years ago. It's taking over pieces of what we used to do. We information professionals were extremely resistant ten years ago to any kind of software front ends, any end-user searching, any giving away of this magical power that we had. But in reality, we were keeping ourselves down. Now that we can teach people to do what we were able to do, we are free to do much more complex research. There shouldn't be any reason for us to grab corporate reports from Dun & Bradstreet [22, see Appendix A]—our constituents can do that themselves. It's not worth our time, it's not worth our salary; we have learned that in the last ten years. So I think the impact is twofold: Technology has helped us, and we have grown in our appreciation of the power of our profession, of our ability to move forward and make ourselves more valuable to our corporations and our constituents.

**Of course, the other enormous factor in how our profession has changed over the past five years is the amount of business information available on the Internet and, consequently, on our constituents' desktops.**

I would say that within the last three years we have been very fortunate in that a lot of our constituents now understand what is and isn't available on the Net. If they even knew what the Web was three years ago, they thought, "It's all out there and it's all free." Now they understand very clearly that it's not all out there, and it's not all free, and it can be very time-consuming to find. This has been the single most encouraging marketing trend that I've seen in the twenty-some years I've been in the field. I don't have to explain to anyone what I do anymore. It's like having a billboard in everyone's living room that says, "Information is online through your computer, and all you have to do is find it yourself or get someone who knows how to find it."

# And people have a much better appreciation for the fact that information can be difficult or time-consuming to find.

Yes, and that is the big change from, say, five years ago. They may not appreciate the skill that it takes, but they do appreciate the amount of knowledge that it takes to find the information efficiently. If they only knew where to go, they could get it. But that's the key. They don't know where to go, and that's where the professional comes in. We can find what they need on a one-time basis, teach them how to do it themselves, set up a "push" system for them, or all three. Again, I think end-user searching has raised the bar on the value of our field, that of the professional business information researcher.

# Do you run into many clients who say "I already did an Internet search, so please don't get the stuff that I found there. What else can you find for me since I already searched the whole Web?"

Oh, yes. And it's kind of sad, in a way. Let's go back five years. Even though it was expensive, a lot of people had desktop access to Dow Jones [21], for example. They'd say, "Well, I already searched the newspapers and there's nothing there." You're faced with two issues you have to tactfully raise with your client. Number one: "What, exactly, did you search?" Number two: "I know you're a very, very intelligent consultant on how to open a business in Botswana; however, you're not a full-time researcher, so the fact that you couldn't find anything there might not mean that there isn't any information available. Perhaps we can work as a team on this."

There's nothing I hate hearing more than "I've already done an Internet search." You feel like you're speaking a different language.

The clients don't want me to repeat anything they've done or search anywhere they've searched, but, frankly, I ignore them and do a Net search anyway if I think it makes sense. Of course, I have a few clients who do know their limitations. They're the best clients. They will say, "I did a Yahoo! [60] search. I got seventeen thousand records and I looked at the first forty, and I'm frustrated." Now, that's something I can deal with.

I do think it's getting easier, because there's more appreciation of our profession than there was before. We used to be seen as equivalent to the secretarial pool, and that changed five or six years ago. Now, higher-level management people, especially, are saying, "This is ridiculous, I'm not going to spend my time doing this. I'm going to get someone from the information center to do this research." Quite a few of my colleagues receive calls from clients saying, "We need an information professional for our off-site meeting for three days." They just want an information professional sitting there available to do searches, in the same room with the project team, whatever it is. Sometimes they will also be the recording person, to keep everyone on track and on the agenda, but more often than not they just want them there to do research. So the project team will say, "We need the top ten companies making bicycles in China." Boom-bang, she's off and running on the search, right in the same room, finds the information, prints it out, hands it out, and they move on. It certainly puts the researcher on the spot, but it's a clear indication of the new understanding of the value of a business researcher.

## Let's think about the process of searching, which itself seems to have changed over the past few years, what with our different roles as information massagers, if you will.

# When you get a project, how do you decide where to start?

Well, let's assume that I've already talked to the client to find out what the information will be used for. I've done a really good reference interview and figured out what the client already has. I am very old-fashioned; more often than not I start with a search in PROMT—Dialog [20] file 16—and limit it to the "current" file. I check to see what information is there and what terms seem to work. I display everything in format 8—just the title and indexing terms. I might get a hundred records, but with the Dialog DialUnit pricing structure, there's no reason not to display that many records and spend fifteen or twenty minutes looking through them online.

Then I develop a preliminary search strategy. This usually includes a call back to the client to redefine the question. We get a lot of research projects that are very clear in the client's mind, but when we do some preliminary research, we realize that it's not so clear-cut after all. So I'll call the client back and tell her, for example, that there's a difference between straw and hay, where it's grown and how it's harvested, and then we'll redefine the search to address these additional questions. My next step is usually to hit the Web. I'll look for trade associations, or Web sites dedicated to straw and hay, for example. I try not spend more than half an hour or so browsing the Net at that point.

Then I take the information that I've gathered and, depending on the project, either get on the phone and conduct some telephone research or go back to the for-fee online services—usually the ones where I have flat-fee access, but I am careful with that decision. You can waste so much time in flat-fee searching, it's almost like the Net. You don't have any financial incentive to focus your search.

## That's an interesting thought—the fact that its flat-fee pricing sometimes discourages you from using a service. You need that meter ticking or the DialUnit counter *ka-chunking* away.

It sharpens my concentration. I'm not saying I like to pay transactional prices, but flat-fee pricing has its own problems. It can cause laziness and sloppy searching. I am not saying that it's the vendor's fault; it very well could be my fault, because in the back of my head I'm thinking, "Ha, ha, flat fee, who cares?" I guess I just like the discipline of transactional pricing.

I also find that if I'm on a transactional-pricing system, I get back to the client a lot more quickly, because I'm really efficient when I'm looking at titles and indexing terms in a preliminary search. I can call back and ask, "Did you mean all European leather or only Italian leather?" Transactional pricing makes me think more quickly and move along more quickly.

## What about the other end of the search process? How do you know when to end a search?

Sometimes it's a time problem. The client needs it by noon because his meeting's at three. More often than not, though, it's what I call the full-circle factor, when you start finding the same stuff over again. Granted, I used to believe in that more than I do now. I used to believe I could search several files, talk to several associations, and keep coming up with the same answers. But now, given the plethora of online resources, sometimes I will simply take a pause, get a cup of coffee, and sit and think for a minute. That's a very underrated part of what information professionals do—sitting back and thinking. And it will come to me: "I think I read about a new file that specifically covers nuclear waste sites. Where did I see it? Was it on the Web?"

There's so much out there that I think we have to pause and use our memories, maybe hit the Web again, maybe call a colleague who we know has done research on nuclear waste dump sites. After that final step, I know I've probably gone as far as I can. I will explain to the client that there could be more out there, depending upon the value of the project and the time frame, but that I think I've found a good portion of what's available.

## The hard thing is that, in the past, you could stop when you felt like you'd gone full circle, but the circle is so much bigger now.

That's a good way of explaining it. When we relied only on commercial services, there was a large but limited amount of information available. Now, it's an almost limitless amount of information, what with the Net and specialized niche databases. As a matter of fact, one of the most disheartening and alarming things is that, after you think you've come full circle, you go online again or make a call, and a whole other world opens up. And you think, "Oh my word, now what? I had no idea that this particular institute was tracking this." And it's almost as if you're starting the project over again.

## I think that's the sign of a Super Searcher— that ability to recognize that there *is* a whole other realm of information out there and to gauge which of the information universes, as it were, to search.

A lot of it is instinct too—sometimes you just feel that you haven't hit the right sources yet. It's a combination of the wisdom of having been in the field for a number of years, luck, and suspending disbelief enough to think that there *has* to be more information on this topic.

But you also have to keep the business side of the equation in mind. You can feel in your gut that there's something more out there, but you know that the project just isn't worth it to the company. You might get a question for a speech that someone's giving to the local Chamber of Commerce, and you're asked for something like "How many little boys in this particular town cut themselves and needed disinfectant?" You may know that the information is out there, and you may know you can find it, but you have to weigh the value of spending your time and energy and money on this project against working on another more crucial project.

## Related to the issue of knowing about a specialized database is the question of how you stay up on all these information sources. How do you learn about new niche databases, a new Internet source or new files in the professional online databases?

Usually by mistake. If I'm having trouble finding information, one of the standard things I do is talk to colleagues, and sometimes they'll say, "Well, that's all in file XYZ or in Web site ABC." So you could say I stay updated by word of mouth. In fact, I have recently developed a policy that helps me in the most surprising way. I talk to a lot of information professionals during the course of a typical day. I try now to end the conversation by saying, "Well, I've got to get back to finding out how many Beanie Babies were sold during December." It is amazing to me how often my colleague will direct me to the exact right person or site for help on my project!

I also rely, of course, on reading the professional journals—we all have to do that. I have stacks and stacks of professional reading material waiting for me in my office.

## Having them piled up there doesn't mean you're going to absorb them just through osmosis, Linda.

Whatever happened to putting it under your pillow? Actually, I think professional writing and speaking are two of the best ways to keep up, because speaking or writing requires me to get up to speed on a subject. I know that not everyone has the need, desire or opportunity to do professional writing or speaking, but if you do, that's a really good way to discipline yourself into staying abreast of industry news. I think electronic mailing lists help a lot too. I subscribe to Buslib [63] and AIIP's listserv [61]. Even banter on a listserv can help. Someone will mention a file that I haven't been to in a while and I learn about enhancements to that file.

The other way I am kept up to date is by my clients, who will tell me about something that they got from the last researcher that they worked with. They'll tell me how it was formatted beautifully and it's exactly what they needed for their PowerPoint presentation, for example. So sometimes just being alert, and not being a know-it-all, enables me to learn from clients' comments.

## You can learn a lot from just listening, can't you? On another topic, what are the business information resources that you consider to be your "core collection"—the things you'd need

## if you were stranded on a desert island and, heaven forbid, had to do business research?

In terms of the professional online sources, ABI/Inform—Dialog's file 15—for management issues; the *Encyclopedia of Associations* [78] and a telephone—I'd have to have a cell phone on my desert island. I get enormous amounts of research done through finding the correct contacts. And I like using the commercial press release databases rather than going directly to the company's Web sites. If there has been any news, I know I'll find it in the database, and the company's Web site is always listed on the press release, so you just go from the press release to the Web site.

## Instead of going to the corporate Web site directly for company news?

Yes. The Web sites, as you know, can be very difficult to navigate. A corporate Web site is set up the way *they* want you to discover information about their company. On the other hand, PR Newswire is just a big bunch of press releases—much more straightforward. I can find what I want there. I don't have the time to flip from corporate Web site to corporate Web site looking for the news. I want to find the news first and then hit the Web sites that I think are important.

The Web sites I would want to take with me to a desert island would be, interestingly enough, the major news networks—ABC [1], NBC [44] and CBS.com [12]. I probably would also want to take Amazon.com [3] with me, or the Books in Print [9] database. I would take Dow Jones Interactive, too, but I only need three of their papers: *The New York Times*, *The Wall Street Journal* and *The Washington Post*. That would be all. I think I could do an awful lot of business research with all that.

## Do you use any of the Web search engines much, or do you generally go straight to these other sources that you listed?

I use AltaVista [2] and Yahoo! I don't like them very much, but I use them because I've got them.

## Would you say that most of your searching these days is done through a browser, or are you still using proprietary software or specialized communications software?

I use a browser for Net searching and for Dow Jones Interactive. But I still use Smartcom, an old-fashioned terminal emulation program, for most of my other online searching. I use it exclusively when I search Dialog because I don't like any of Dialog's front ends.

## To shift gears from the search to the output, tell me about the formats in which you are sending out your search results these days. I realized yesterday that I haven't seen my FedEx guy in three weeks because now I'm sending everything electronically. Have you noticed that too?

Yes, absolutely. Everything's sent electronically or—once in a great while—by fax if they're having a technical problem receiving the file. For delivery of Web pages, I do one of two things: If I'm working at a client's site, I provide a link, because they can get it through their network. If I'm not, I just give them the Web site's URL. I don't screen-capture pages, but I do sometimes download pages and then convert them into Microsoft Word if the formatting works, and then I send it to them in Microsoft Word, noting the Web site URL.

**What I sometimes do is create a hidden Web page with all the URLs and any annotations I want to add, and load that page on my Web site. I don't list the client's name on the page, and I don't link it to any of my other pages, so it's essentially an invisible Web page. I give the address to my client, and he can go directly to the page and view or print or download the individual sites. Then I delete it in a couple of days to make sure that it doesn't get picked up by any of the search engine robots. So I guess Web delivery is another one of our value-added services.**

**Speaking of delivering Web sites to clients, how do you deal with the reliability of information that you get from the Web? Do most of your clients understand that this is something that you may or may not be able to retrieve again later?**

I almost never provide a client with anything from the Web unless it is an association, university or corporate Web site. But if I do, I make it very, very clear that this is not a Web site that can be verified as being correct, but they asked about almonds and cancer, and here's where I found things about almonds and cancer. I will include Web information if I'm already familiar with the site, or I'll make a phone call to find out. And if I get a recording saying, "Hi, this is Bob and we're out of the office," that Web site doesn't go to my client. But if I can track down the Web site owner and make sure that it actually is the University of Kansas or whatever, as it claims to be, I'll send it to them. I'm not in the business of distinguishing the wheat from the chaff of what's on the Web, so my World Wide Web is a very, very *small* world. I'm pretty strict about what I will recommend to my clients.

# Can you describe a research project that was particularly fun or interesting? Something that you can look back on and say, "Yes, this is why I keep doing this."

There's one I just finished that was really fun and is a good example of what I like most about business research. There's a building boom in Hawaii, and a lot of the West Coast home-building companies are flying across the Pacific Ocean to build homes there. When I started this project, I didn't even know that there were huge home-building companies all over the country that are publicly traded. The National Association of Home Builders can provide lists of all kinds of information. I learned that you need special permits if your home-building company is located in one state and you're building in another state, for example, and there's a whole lot of intrigue involved in getting permits. I learned a lot; that's what made this such an interesting project.

What I love most is when I get my hands around a project on a topic that I don't know much about. One I did a few years ago that I loved was about milk prices. Why are milk prices regulated and what does that mean to the small dairy farmer? I got paid to learn about why milk prices are regulated. For people with a curious mind, it's great that you can wake up, bounce out of bed and say to your husband, "I'm going to learn more about why milk prices are regulated!" "Yes, dear. Bye-bye." Non-researchers just don't get it!

Here's another one I enjoyed: Did you know that there are more U.S. dollars in circulation in the former Soviet Union than there are in the United States? The United States actually spent more time explaining about the new $20 bills in our overseas currency offices than they did here in the United States. In a lot of countries, U.S. currency is used as "hard currency," and people would see the new $20 bills and think that they were counterfeit.

Of course, I've had projects I hate too. They're so boring you could fall asleep doing them. Lists are especially bad. "Get me market-share data, market penetration, market size and sales channels of washing machines in Italy, France, Germany and the U.K." Jobs like that are tedious, they're annoying, they're always incomplete, and you've got to look at one million sources to pull together the data. It's the kind of thing that the client usually thinks is right there at the push of a button. I wish more clients would ask me to find out why there are more U.S. dollars in Russia than here. *That* I'm interested in.

# What frustrates me is when all a client wants is a couple of articles on a topic that I think is really interesting, and I want to say, "No, I can't stop now!"

No, you must know more about Charles DeGaulle! You have to know more! "No, I only want one line for a speech." No! Of course, what's tricky is when a client asks for something that he thinks is simple and straightforward but that actually requires a lot of work. The client is going to France to give a speech introducing a new product. So he asks me for quotes from Charles DeGaulle. My first inclination is to ask, why Charles DeGaulle? It probably means that over dinner his wife said, "You should quote Charles DeGaulle." So he calls me and says, "I need a Charles DeGaulle quote for my speech in France to introduce product ABC." "Why Charles DeGaulle?" "Well, just Charles

DeGaulle." "What about?" "Doesn't matter." So I'm getting a Charles DeGaulle quote that might be totally inappropriate, but the client's not willing to let me consult with him to find out if Charles DeGaulle is the right or the wrong person. Maybe it should be Napoleon. Instead, all he wants from me is a collection of quotes; he doesn't want my recommendations on other sources who might be more appropriate.

So you go through all this and you come up with ten quotes from Charles DeGaulle, and it takes you three or four hours. You give them to him, and he says, "I don't understand the context of this." Well, that's because you didn't read all the stuff that I read. "And why did this take four hours?"

This ties in to the effect of the Web on information availability. People used to be amazed if you could come up with two Charles DeGaulle quotes in two days. Now they're annoyed if you come up with ten in two hours and none of them seems to be right. They think it's all out there on the Web, it's all free, and you just push a button.

Another part of the problem is figuring out when the client *really* needs the information—when it's truly a rush request and when it's not. Every business client says he wants the information right now. So I'll take in the research request, I'll think about it a few minutes, I'll practically slit my throat over how boring it is, and then I'll call the client back and say, "Well, I've made some progress, but what I need to know is, will this information be as valuable tomorrow afternoon as it would be today?" And the client will say, "Sure, my speech is not for a month."

## Any other search tips that you've found especially useful?

The reference interview is the most important part of any search—absolutely, bar none. The preliminary search is the next most important, a quick search where I print off some records in format 8 on Dialog to get the terminology and understand what's happened in the last six months. And the follow-up interview is the third most important part, after you've done a preliminary search. You get yourself a little bit smarter on the research topic, then you call the client back and review any unresolved issues on the topic.

Then I do the search and print the results in a streamlined format—usually just the bibliographic citation and the text but no indexing terms or abstract—and highlight a few key sentences or paragraphs. After that, I write an introductory executive summary of less than a page, if what I am providing for them is a set of search results. If I'm providing them with what I would call *information*, they never see the search results per se. They see my analysis, which is just a report pulling out charts and graphs and quotes that I've gotten from the articles, with footnotes back to the original sources.

My other Super Searcher tip is to remind business searchers that we're not searchers, we're researchers. This has changed in the last few years, and we all have to remember it. We are finally providing information and not search results. We have more features now, just as our search tools do. Spreadsheets are great. Clients love it when you line up the companies and say they've introduced new products in these countries and they've invested this much in advertising here and there (you know, we're in a PowerPoint world), and they like to take that stuff, slam it into their presentations and move on.

Of course, it also depends on your relationship with your clients. If you're working *for* a team, I think you should give them something that's usable in the format in which you present it. If you're *on* a team, you can sit together and say, "Well, here's the search results that I have. Where do you want to go from here?" And sometimes they'll have someone who's more skilled at putting together the graph or whatever. But if they expect something professional from you, you've got to think about what they're using it for. Are they giving a presentation? Are they putting it in a report? Is it for their spouse or child? Is it for their boss? Our presentation of search results is so much more sophisticated and varied these days than what it used to be. The formatting is almost as important as the research itself.

## What do you see down the road for information professionals?

After watching the changes in our field during my career, I'd be afraid to speculate. From 300-baud ASCII and, what, twenty online files, to this? One of the things that amuses me about online searching is that, in the beginning, we all had to be so careful about the time we spent online. We would prepare for a search like a runner stretching before a 10-K race. In my first job, at ISI, we worked in an open space in the library. We didn't want patrons interrupting us during precious, expensive, scary online searching. So we set up a sign when we went online. It said, "If the red light on the modem is lit, do not disturb the librarian." Ha! And now, with flat-fee contracts and all-you-can-eat Web access, I quite often stay logged on all day. I'll even walk away from a search to fill my coffee cup. Dialog's Logoff Hold command is pretty obsolete now, and it used to be my lifesaver.

I am looking forward to the changes we will see. Many information professionals are still worrying that their careers will be obsolete. I think we will continue to see the opposite. I am reminded of Mead Corp., the paper company, which froze in its tracks when it first heard the phrase "the paperless office" and immediately went into the electronic world with Lexis-Nexis. Computers produce paper at a zillion times the rate that typewriters did!

It's the same with our field. Our constituents know more about, and better appreciate, our skills now that the curtain has been raised for them on what we actually do. Momma, send your babies to library school.

# Super Searcher Power Tips

▶   When I'm searching, I'm really doing it for myself, because the deliverable is no longer the search output but an analysis of the search results.

▶   The reference interview is the most important part of any search.

▶   The preliminary search is very important—a quick search where I've printed off some records in format 8 on Dialog to get the terminology and understand what's happened in the last six months.

▶   Rely on your colleagues to help you stay current on available resources. Water cooler chat is a part of our job.

▶   We're not searchers, we're researchers. We are providing information, not search results.

# Helene Kassler

## Competitive Intelligence Expert

Helene Kassler is the director of Library and Information Services at Fuld & Co. in Cambridge, MA. In addition to online research, she trains Fuld staff and clients and is a frequent speaker on competitor intelligence.

hkassler@fuld.com
www.fuld.com/i3

## First, tell me a little bit about your background and how you wound up in competitive intelligence.

I started out professionally as a journalist. I have a master's degree in journalism, and I worked as a science journalist focusing on energy conservation for about ten years. I finally came to the conclusion that I didn't like the writing anywhere near as much as I loved the research. I would go to the library to write my articles and just get lost in the books. So after burning out on writing, I kept thinking, "I really want to do research, I really want to do research." At the time I wasn't fully aware of corporate libraries. People kept saying, "Oh, you could be a fact checker, you could do this, you could do that." I decided to network with information professionals to see what options were available. Radcliffe's career resource center offered an afternoon session on alternative careers for librarians. An information broker was there and gave a presentation and really struck a chord with me. I thought "This is it; this is what I want to do." I talked with her afterwards, and she explained that an M.L.S. degree was my union card for this business, so I went and got my M.L.S. from Simmons.

I knew that I wanted to go into the business world. I took a course in business literature that was taught by Prof. Jerry Miller, who focused on competitor intelligence. One of the requirements was to do a CI project for a company—not for your brother-in-law, not for yourself. My undergraduate focus was on genetics, and there were quite a few biotech companies in Boston. I went to one of the poor, struggling biotech firms that couldn't afford to pay for a professional CI project, and did a free competitor intelligence project for them. Jerry Miller was just blown away by the report, and the biotech company loved it too. As it turned out, the national SCIP [96, see Appendix A] conference was in Boston that year, and Jerry told me to take my resumé and network at the conference.

I talked to people from Fuld & Company at their booth and gave them my resumé. A couple of months later, I got a call and was told that they were looking for someone to do part-time library work. I was interested. When I came in for an interview, they asked me to bring examples of my literature searching that wasn't just for a class project. All I had was the CI project I'd done for Jerry Miller's class. When they saw it, they said, "Do you know that this was a multi-thousand-dollar project that you did for them?" And I said, "Oh, yeah, Jerry thought it was pretty good." They told me that they were looking for researchers more than librarians—that they were afraid they'd have to turn away clients because they didn't have enough researchers. So I agreed to work as a researcher on a health-care project. My love was still library research, doing online research. When that project was finished, I moved over to working with the librarian. She left after a while, and I became the full-time librarian. Having worked on those research projects gave me a really good grounding in CI research.

The other important part of this story is that when I was going to Simmons, Web browsers weren't around yet. We used gophers, telnet, ftp, and email, but the Web didn't really make headlines until 1995. When I came to Fuld, we used CompuServe a bit when we needed to search databases for non-billable proposal work, so we were already starting to use alternative sources for information. But then Netscape landed when I was at Fuld, and we thought, "Hey, it looks like there's some information out there that could be useful." We started looking into some of the Usenet groups and at company home pages. Also early on in my work at Fuld, Michael Sandman, the senior vice president, asked me to go into Dialog [20] and pull down a 10-K report on a company. I said, "I believe I can get it for free on EDGAR [23]." I'd learned that from Jerry Miller's class, when he brought in an email announcement he'd just received about SEC filings being available on a trial basis on the Net.

So that's how I started using the Net. At that point in early 1995, it involved less creativity. It was more along the lines of just being able to find a company Web site or retrieve an SEC filing [54]. I remember back in late 1994, we were doing a project on a pharmaceutical company and trying to piece together their strategic plans for a certain drug. The company didn't have a Web page up, but a couple of months later I came upon one they had finally put up, and there was a good portion of the strategic plan. Of course, you don't find strategic plans on the Web as often now. But the Web really revolutionized how we do our jobs. I don't know if traditional business researchers have had the same experience, but for competitor intelligence, it has really changed what we do and how we do it.

As competitor intelligence consultants, we get hired by a lot of major companies asking us to find information that isn't published. If the information were readily available, the client would have found it without our help. So we need to go after what we call the primary resources—experts in the field, reporters, editors, associations, staff members, even building inspectors and people like that who have more knowledge than they ever put in their printed reports.

**What I find so unusual about CI work is that you're identifying people who have information that they don't even realize is useful. Most business researchers are looking for an expert on widgets, they find the widget expert and they talk about widgets. But you're talking to someone like a building inspector who may have no idea that the information in his head is so valuable to you.**

Yes, that's very true. There are numerous government agencies—EPA and OSHA, for example—whose employees and reports can be very informative on facilities and chemicals. In one case, we were able to buy a videotape inspection of a factory, giving us tremendous detail about the equipment used.

We also turn to journalists as sources of information. I think it's been said that only twenty percent of the information reporters or journalists gather is put in print; they're an incredible untapped resource. Conference speakers are another great resource. It used to be time-consuming to track down speakers and ask for their notes. Now, you go on the Web, you find the conference or you put together the company name, conference and speaker, and if it's a really broad subject, you put in the topic. Not only can you find the conference speakers and contact them through their email addresses now, but they're often putting their PowerPoint presentations up on a Web site. We can look at the presentation and then call them and say, "Gee, we had a question about the left wing nut on the widget in your presentation." So the Net has really facilitated how we go about gathering information.

Our online charges are as high as they've ever been, but our company has grown quite a bit too. So, ultimately, there have been savings from the Internet. But more importantly, we've gained easy access to some resources that were once hard to locate—job postings, resumés, industry statistics from associations, and so on. We now start research on the Internet, whereas we used to start on the professional online services. We'll begin with SEC filings and company home pages, which can be incredibly rich sources of information.

## Can you give an example of a typical CI research project?

We had a client who was interested in the information technology—the hardware and software—being used in beverage production. Companies are strongly interested in what technologies their competitors are implementing. Our first step was to go to computer publications, some of the databases on Dialog. At that time we were doing mostly Dialog searching; we've now switched to mostly Dow Jones [21] searching. So we pulled up some articles and found one or two mentions of some software applications used in the manufacturing, but we didn't find a whole lot, and the articles didn't provide much description.

Since I wasn't finding much, I took the software vendors' names that we did turn up, combined them with the target company and looked them up on the Net. Believe it or not, we actually found what hardware the vendors' software ran on, along with other manufacturing information that told us what hardware the company was using.

One of the vendors had an excellent Web site full of information on its diagnostic equipment. The vendor posted a success story about its relationship with one manufacturing facility in our research project. It described how much was produced at the site, which lines were produced, who produced the cardboard packaging, and what kind of container was the biggest seller. The vendor offered these incredible particulars to promote its capabilities. While I often find the greatest detail about companies and facilities in local press, this went way beyond what the local press would cover.

# That sounds like another example of finding information put out by someone who has no idea how valuable the information is.

That's right. We often look for information from related parties—suppliers' press releases announcing contracts, hyperlinks between alliance partners, client lists, that sort of thing. Each bit of information is another piece of the puzzle we fit together in our CI research projects.

Some people denigrate the value of what's on the Internet, saying "Oh, it's only advertisements." But advertising is valuable because it's what the company wants to hype. And years ago, if we wanted to get a brochure from a company, we'd have to jump through all these hoops about why did we want it, who were we and how valid was our need, how long would it take for us to get it, and so on. Now we just get the information from the company's Web site, no questions asked.

The same thing is true with association Web sites; they can be really useful for industry statistics, things like that. Years ago, you'd call an association and, though they were nice, if you got anything at all from them—if you found anyone who'd *speak* to you—you were doing well.

The downside of all of this, of course, is that the Internet has made *everything* so much faster. Clients want things much faster, so requests that used to have a week turn-around time are now "by the end of the day."

My latest favorite trick when I'm doing this kind of research is to look up reverse links—a search to see what Web pages link *to* a particular company's site. When I find a smaller site that doesn't link to very many places outside, with no suggestions of who they're affiliated with, I search HotBot [31] or AltaVista [2] to find who's linked to the site.

## Can you go into more detail on how you do this reverse link look-up?

It's sort of like a reverse telephone number look-up. In HotBot, you pull down the option for "all the words" and select "links to this URL." In AltaVista, you use the *link* prefix, so to find links to the Fuld Web site, for example, you'd search *link:www.fuld.com*.

In the beverage project I just described, I searched for links to the software vendor and found some of the affiliated hardware applications. In another project, we were looking at a smaller subsidiary of a very large company in the service sector. But the small company had the most meager Web page you can imagine—I think my nephew has a better one—and they were very stingy with what they were giving out. We found almost no links pointing outward from them. I did a reverse link lookup, and we found a number of government programs in which they participated and offered discounts for their services. We spoke with government employees who were able to provide more information about the company, their services and discounts. Government programs are part of the public record, but most people don't think about them.

## How would you have identified that government contact otherwise?

It would have been hard. We did literature searches; the company never announced that they were part of a government program. We pored over their Web site and didn't find anything there, either. It's an interesting phenomenon—a small vendor that sells something to a large, recognized company will often publicize the contract. In some cases, the information is so revealing, it looks to me like they haven't checked with their client first. That's often been how we find out what kind of information technology a company is using.

I see this kind of non-approved information, too, in the *Wall Street Transcript* [58]. It's a riot! The mid-level managers are told, "Don't divulge our strategic plans" and then the CEO is interviewed for *Wall Street Transcript* and says, "Here's our five-year plan." It's the same reason that I like the CNBC/Dow Jones Business Video service [17]. It has audio and video recordings of interviews with government officials and company officials archived for 90 days. You can set up an alert so that, when somebody from a company you're interested in is going to be interviewed, you get an email alert. You never know what wonderful information they'll let slip in a freewheeling interview.

# What other CI information do you look for on the Net?

I have a feeling that we've publicized it a little too much, but job postings have historically been wonderful sources of information. Before the Internet, there were two options for getting job postings. One was to subscribe to the local press or the trade press and see what jobs a company posted, and two, there used to be a company that tracked classified ads—but I'm fairly certain they're out of business now; I think the Web killed them.

For job postings, companies are strongly vested in not getting swamped with a million resumés. So they want to be specific about what they're looking for. The more specific they get, the more technical information they give us. A few years ago, we were looking for information on a privately held high-tech company. We weren't sure how many employees it had, and we were also looking at the technologies it was using. We looked in every publication and directory you could think of, but couldn't find useful information anywhere. I went into Deja News [19], which searches the Usenet newsgroups. It's unrealistic to subscribe to all the potentially relevant Usenet groups. But Deja News does a wonderful job of searching through the newsgroups that they archive, including the *jobs.offered* ones. As it turns out, the company we were researching listed fifteen or twenty positions in one posting on *houston.jobs.offered* and *us.jobs.offered*. And the job posting reported that they had seven thousand employees in Omaha, Nebraska and Texas. It listed the positions and skills they were looking for—COBOL, C, Unix, VI Editor, SQL, shell scripting, TCP/IP, Dialogic, and so on. Our project manager looked at the posting and said, "Well, this tells me the hardware and software configuration they're using in their operations. This is just what we were looking for."

That was back in 1996, and it prompted us to use the job postings quite aggressively. Our recent experience is that companies are not posting very thorough job ads on the Web or in Usenet groups anymore. They're saying, "If you're interested in a marketing position, call us. If you're interested in information technology, call us."

## Have you noticed the same phenomenon in non-U.S. job postings?

I was recently working on a presentation for the Internet Librarian conference, and I wanted to show a foreign job posting with some good detailed information. I tried Deja News, I was in CareerMosaic [11], I was in Monster Board [42], I went into some Yahoo! [60] areas, I went into some French stuff, because I can speak a little *Français*. I spent so much time, I was pulling my hair out looking for a good example. And finally I thought, "Why don't I try a large company Web site?" And I'm thinking, "This is crazy, if this works I'm going to jump out the window, because I just wasted two hours getting fancy rather than going straight to the company Web page." So I picked Alcatel, went to the Alcatel Web site at www.alcatel.com, and sure enough—they've got job postings specifying the information technologies they're using.

We also search for resumés when we're looking for competitive intelligence on a company. We'll try to contact former employees and say, "We don't want you to break any confidentiality agreements, but is there anything you can talk about?" We also look at their online resumés to see what they say they've done at their last job. Sometimes, resumés give research details or specific examples of technologies in use.

## When you look for local press coverage of a company, what online service do you use?

We typically use Dow Jones for local press. It is so easy to focus in by state and then by city if you need to. Pricing is a factor too—we bill for both our time and our online services, and a flat fee is completely unacceptable for us, because we really don't know how much work we're going to do in any month. One month we might be over, one month we might be under. How do you bill clients appropriately?

Not long ago, we were mainly a Dialog shop. But now, we're finding very good information on Dow Jones, finding it a lot easier, and seeing fewer duplicates. So we naturally have changed; our first choice now is Dow Jones, and Dialog is second. But I have a great example of local press coverage we weren't able to find on either Dialog or Dow Jones. We were looking for a pilot energy project up in New Hampshire. At the time—this was a couple of years ago—the Manchester *Union Leader* was supposed to be on Dow Jones. I went in and I found nothing on the project. So then I tried searching on the word "Clinton," and I found nothing on Clinton.

## That's a good reality check, isn't it?

Yep. I realized that, although they claimed they were on Dow Jones, they weren't. So I went looking for the Manchester *Union Leader's* Web site, since it was supposedly the only newspaper in

New Hampshire on the Web. It turns out that their Web site was still under development. So we just put the company name, the name of the pilot project and "New Hampshire" in a search engine and turned up a small community paper from a coastal town in New Hampshire. It turns out that it was one of the cities involved in the pilot project, and the paper had interviewed some local people involved in the pilot. We called the people interviewed and they answered some of our questions. So this was one case where what we needed wasn't on the professional online services. Then again, there are things in the professional online services that aren't on the Net. You can never do one and not the other.

**I think a lot of us tend to use only the professional online services when we want to search a number of newspapers. Just the thought of searching fifteen newspapers on the Net gives me hives because of the time involved. But we forget to try the Net if we can't find the papers we want on the professional online services.**

And it's only going to get worse, because some periodicals are now only available on the Web. Plus major providers like *Financial Times* are pulling their content from commercial services and offering access only via their own Web site. It's really the Wild West for us information professionals. Another challenge is that the Net has grown so much that it's hard to know what's out there, and you want to pull your hair out. The bigger the Net gets, the better Yahoo! looks, excluding garbage and organizing sites into a comfortable hierarchy.

# Do you find that you rely more on your established bookmarks or Yahoo! when you begin a search, or do you start with one of the giant search engines like AltaVista or HotBot?

It really depends on the questions asked. Our projects can center on pricing, distribution, manufacturing, advertising, and research. You name it, we've probably done it. I'm not sure there's a typical path for our information gathering. For certain things I know where to go—for example, job postings, SEC filings, news stories, computer information, and associations. If it's an industry-specific question and I know some good sites, I'll go there first. Or I'll look for an association in ASAE's [4] site.

OK, do you want to hear my Ph.D. thesis on the use of search engines? It's just so hard to keep up. I prefer HotBot as my first search engine, but I set up Netscape to not accept cookies and HotBot requires a lot of cookies. I keep trying AltaVista, but I'm not convinced that the power search combined with the relevancy ranking features work very well. I've talked to Greg Notess [91] about it, and I'm just not convinced that it's really doing a relevancy ranking. I like Northern Light's [47] relevancy ranking and its custom folders.

The most critical thing is knowing your search engines and knowing how they work. Until I went to the search engine conference in Boston, "Search Engines and Beyond," I didn't know that some search engines did word-for-word searches, and some of them were concept matching or statistical mapping. If you're doing squishy concept searching, forget AltaVista and HotBot, because they're doing word-for-word matching, and they can't figure out what a concept is. When you're getting a gazillion hits in AltaVista and you realize, well, this is a little squishy, then you need to take the search to a search engine that handles relevancy ranking and concept searching. Northern Light, with its the custom folders, will help focus and sort a search, and Excite [25] seems to do a very good job with concepts. I also like Excite's "more like this" feature, which locates pages that statistically match the original. If you find a page you like, this feature often finds more. I also use Yahoo! for some oddball kinds of things. You're given the name of a very small company and you're asked for some of the company's competitors, for example. Put it in Yahoo! and figure out what category the company falls under and then look at all the other companies listed in that category.

If you're looking for the home page of a good-sized company, Excite is very good because it puts an entire company profile up at the top of the search results list. When it's a very small company, I like the company locator service that Net Partners [45] has. It's based on InterNIC's [36] domain registration. That's a great way of figuring out who owns a company or a Web site—by looking at the Internet domain registration information.

To get back to the search engines, I'll start with HotBot, especially if the search strategy is simple. When it starts getting more and more complex, I find that AltaVista handles the most complicated searches with Boolean logic the best. On the other hand, I do like the way the results come up on HotBot, and I like its meta-tag and concept searching. So it's a wild ride, what can I say?

## It is. It feels like every six months everything you know is wrong and you have to start all over again.

For the last three years I've gone to the Online World conference, and every single time I hear Greg Notess speak, I change search engines. I call him my search engine guru. So the last time I saw him, I said, "OK, Greg, what search engine are you using now?" He said, "All of them." I said, "Thank you. That's what I do now too."

It's so exasperating. You'll do a search, you'll have used the proper terms, and you get all of this garbage. That's when the value of something like Yahoo! comes in. They don't accept the garbage—they just eliminate it. So again, it's know thy search engine—what it does, how it works, what it doesn't do. Find the specialty search engines and databases that suit your research, because if you're in a certain industry, you've got to know all of those industry-specific periodicals' and organizations' Web sites. You've got to sign up for the news alerts they offer. Sometimes the job postings and resumés will be at those organizational sites when they're not anywhere else.

## It sounds like you have to be proactive in Web searching. You have to find your niche sites ahead of time because it takes a while to sign up for all the news sources and alerting services. But what do you do when you're searching on an industry you haven't researched before and your client needs the information tomorrow?

In our situation, you pick an industry and we've done it. I used to say "Well, one day we're doing pharmaceuticals, the next day we're doing energy." Now, it's "One hour we're doing pharmaceuticals, the next hour we're doing energy." The single resource we use the most is the *Encyclopedia of Business Information Sources* [79]. When you're all over the map like we are, you can't have it all in your head. You can look in some of the periodical directories and you find that biotechnology has twenty pages of listings, whereas the *Encyclopedia of Business Information Sources* may list the top five for you.

## What do you do when you don't have any idea where to start a search?

There are two librarians in our center, Samantha Chmelik and me, and Samantha is absolutely outstanding. So if one of us is having trouble, we'll talk to the other one. We have somewhat complementary backgrounds, so that works pretty well. We both really enjoy what we're doing, because competitive intelligence often deals with products and we love dealing with tangible items. It doesn't matter what—we just find it interesting. You're talking about some unique sector of the tire industry; we find it interesting. We are both fascinated by companies. I view companies as having personalities, and you have to uncover their characteristics. I think most of us in this industry are information junkies.

# Speaking of which, how do you stay on top of developments in the information industry? You use Greg Notess as the *Good Housekeeping* seal of approval for the search engines you use. How else do you keep updated?

The Buslib [63] listserv is wonderful. Samantha and I read it, but generally we're lurkers. Sometimes we may want to post something, but it might tip our hand as to who we're doing research for. I love Buslib because of the number of people who will say, "Yes, I tried that service and it was great," or "Yes, I tried that service and it was awful." And I think a number of vendors can attest to the power of Buslib. The sharing of information that goes on is just phenomenal.

As for the publications we get, we subscribe to *Online* [92], *Database* [77], *Searcher* [94], *CyberSkeptic's Guide* [76], *Information Advisor* [86] and *Information Today* [88], and we try to keep up with them. The busier we get, the harder it gets. And we find *Industry Standard* [84] fascinating in terms of where the Internet's going. We've had a lot of projects involving e-commerce lately—it's really fascinating the way our topics change every couple of years. We also subscribe to Danny Sullivan's Search Engine Watch [65] for information on new search engines and new features from our favorite old search engines.

We also recently signed up for Outsell's E-brief [64] to keep up with the information industry.

## Do you get many clients telling you they've already searched the Net and asking you what else could possibly be available?

We don't get that very often. Most of our users know that we have access to additional information through the professional online services and know that we are top-notch Internet searchers. But there are so many end-user systems out there, and vendors are going after the enterprise-wide market. So I see our role really changing; the searches we're doing are more complex now. Our users will come to us and say, "Oh, I went over the entire company Web site, I have all the SEC filings, I have all the press releases, now what else can you get me?" We also train our end users, keeping them aware of how the search engines have changed and what new resources or techniques we've discovered.

As information professionals, we're going to be more involved in knowledge management, vendor and service assessment, and negotiation. You certainly don't want to leave it to the IS/IT department to negotiate the enterprise-wide contract with your favorite major online vendor, or to decide which services to acquire. Otherwise, they'll say "we can get by with only one of the top three information sources, we don't need the other two, because this one offers the lowest price." We want to make sure end users understand that, while we're putting quality information on their desktops, as information professionals we are still able to provide more high-end, high-value information. Plus, with the Web it seems like an ever-expanding universe of information. It's like that potato chip ad with Jay Leno—"Don't worry ... we'll make more!" There will always be more resources to discover, more techniques to develop, and more change around every corner.

# Super Searcher Power Tips

▶ The most critical thing is knowing your search engines and knowing how they work. Find the specialty search engines and databases that suit your research.

▶ These days, we start research on the Internet, whereas we used to start on the professional online services. Company home pages are incredibly rich sources of information.

▶ My favorite trick when I'm looking at a Web site is to look up reverse links—a search to see what Web pages link to a particular company's site.

▶ Some people denigrate the value of what's on the Internet, saying, "Oh, it's only advertisements," but advertising is valuable because it's what the company wants to hype.

# Susan Klopper

## Wide-Spectrum Business Searcher

Susan Klopper is the Director of the Atlanta Information Center for Arthur Andersen LLP.

susan.m.klopper@arthurandersen.com

## Tell me about your background and how you wound up where you are today professionally.

This is actually a second career for me. I did museum curatorial work for about eight years and got burned out on that. At some point I finally realized that I had to make some money. Believe it or not, there are actually very respectable careers where they make considerably less, even, than librarians. Museum work happened to be one of them. So I went to library school and knew that I definitely wanted to work in a corporate library. My first library job was at CNN where I was the corporate librarian. I was there for just under a year, and that was the most phenomenal first job I could have had. I always knew I wanted to do research, and there I had all this cutting-edge technology.

The job was very fast-paced, very exciting, very demanding, very multitasking, lots of pressure—all the things I thrived under. I got to spend all day long on Dialog [20, see Appendix A] and Lexis [40]; there were really no money constraints. CNN had a remarkable reference collection as well. A lot of the work we did was electronic, which was particularly noteworthy since this was back in 1984, but I also learned to use print reference tools.

Then the friend who had helped me find the job at CNN called and told me about a job at Arthur Andersen. I knew I wanted to manage a library. I was already a bit older, then, than other people coming out of library school, so this was an opportunity to move into a different type of corporate environment and to manage a library as well. I remember thinking that it would be wonderful to actually have time to *think* about the research request—the deadlines at CNN were 30 seconds. But it's all relative. Things still move pretty fast here. I have to warn job applicants that, if they really like to think something through all the way, this is not the place for them. It just doesn't happen. Anyway, I started at Arthur Andersen in 1985 and I'm still there.

## Tell me about your job now. What kind of business research do you do and who are your main clients?

It's a very diverse group. We support all the practices at Arthur Andersen. My information center still provides research for Andersen Consulting, too. We support what I consider the technical practices, main line audit and tax, so we are a quasi-law library. We do, or assist with, a lot of tax and legal research and technical accounting research. But we're also a corporate business library, and in that sense, I don't think there's anything we don't do. We do research on companies, mergers and acquisitions, roll-out of products, strategic issues, and gathering information on the officers and directors of a company and on its competitors.

We do a lot of industry information—trends, forecasts, market share information, finding out who the key players are. We do a tremendous amount of topical research, anything from knowledge management to enterprise resource planning and benchmarking return on investment. Just today we were doing some work on how companies transition from having individual printers, copiers and fax machines all over the place to combining those with digital network printers. So it really runs the gamut. We also gather a lot of financial information—bonds, stocks, exchange rates—and demographic and statistical data on a city or a foreign country.

# Sometimes when I tell people that I do business research, they say "Oh, that's such a narrow focus." And I want to laugh. If it was any broader than this, I think my brain would explode. It's a completely different industry every day, depending on who picks up the phone and calls you.

That's exactly right. And what makes it fascinating is that we may get the same question or the same type of question several times over the course of a day or a week or a month but, depending on the person who's asking it and the group that person is with, it can be a very different question each time. It sounds the same when it comes out of the client's mouth, but when you put all the pieces together, it's clear that you're going to handle the request very differently. It might be the same question, but they get a different answer.

# Can you walk me through an example of a research request you've done recently?

We were asked to gather some information on a specific department store, including the basic financial background. We pulled the 10-K, the annual report, and then we went back a couple of years and located some articles and a couple of pretty juicy analysts' reports. But then the client said he also wanted to understand the specialty department store industry, not only in terms of the overall makeup of the industry, but also the business processes of that industry. This question was coming from somebody in our business-consulting practice, so he needed to understand the big picture and what makes this industry run, and he also needed to understand the functions, the processes that are in place.

We did the easy part first—we pulled reports from our *Standard & Poor's Industry Survey* [55] CD-ROM, from the *US Industry & Trade Outlook* [100], from the WEFA *Industrial Monitor* [59] CD-ROM, and we did some quick online searching for articles on the industry to get a feel for the trends and hot issues.

But we also needed to understand how the industry works from the inside, so we turned to the *Encyclopedia of Associations* [78] on CD-ROM. We quickly identified the National Retail Federation as being a key association, contacted them, and they gave us some guidance to some other sources. Then we used Books in Print [9] and Amazon.com [3] to find any general books on the industry. We particularly looked for books that had a heavy accounting and finance thrust, because they were more likely to discuss the internal processes of the industry, and we ended up ordering two books for the client. By that point, he was pretty pleased and almost overwhelmed with the amount of information we had been able to push out in about four hours.

# You're using a lot of different sources. This isn't just going onto Dialog, throwing in the company name and shipping out whatever comes out the other end.

Right, although that's part of it. That's the fun of the game, I think, having to decide. You've got so many sources to choose from, and you have to figure out the best ones.

# The sources you mentioned are available on a number of different media—online, on CD-ROM, directly on a vendor's Web site, in

# print, and so on. How do you decide which one to use?

We have a very large CD-ROM collection in my information center. I like CD-ROMs; they're cost-effective, they're fast. The ones we collect have good, powerful search engines. For all those reasons, if we've got it on CD-ROM, I will generally gravitate there. Quite honestly, some sources I never consider searching on Dialog. For example, the *Encyclopedia of Associations* has been on Dialog forever, and I would never have imagined searching it on Dialog. I don't know why. Before we had the CD-ROM, we would just go to the print source because the print is so easy to use and it has all those indexes.

I happen to be one of those people who do not think CD-ROM is going to go away. I think it will play a very important role as our classic online systems fade away, which I suspect they will in time. Granted, I jump online when I need to search across lots of varied content. But we have the IntelliSeek, ABI/Inform and Business & Industry databases on CD-ROM, so if I know that the CD-ROM covers the time frame I need, I generally gravitate toward that versus going online. That's even more the case now because the online services have gotten so expensive.

# Do you charge back for your time and/or for the database charges in whatever format you use?

We charge a fixed rate for our service, based on time. In addition, if we incur any hard costs for any of the services we use, we pass that along as well. We don't inflate those costs. We do not charge for the use of CD-ROMs; that's an overhead that my budget absorbs, although it is allocated out across the board to the practice groups.

# Have you seen that the availability of information on the Internet has changed how you do searching? Do you use the Internet for things now that you wouldn't have been able to do a few years ago?

I definitely take advantage of information, for example, that associations might have posted on the Internet, although the quality varies greatly. There's no consistency; sometimes when you least expect it, you'll find a gold mine of information from one organization, and then you find that other associations don't have much of anything.

I take advantage of sources that give me the information more quickly than I could get it by picking up the phone and calling, or by doing a search in Dialog and hoping that nuggets of their studies are captured in articles. I use company Web sites, although I think most of them are a bit overrated in terms of useful information. But our users expect us to go to the company sites, so we do visit those.

We certainly take advantage of the SEC filings, although we don't use the free site that the SEC maintains; we subscribe to Disclosure's Global Access [28]. It's faster, and we need copies of the annual reports as well as 10-Ks. Also, the accounting side of our business requires that we be able to search the full text of the annual reports and SEC filings, and you can't do that on the SEC's EDGAR site [23].

I think the Internet is a very surprising creature, but I certainly don't overestimate its power relative to the other tools that we're accustomed to using. It does have nuggets of information that you either couldn't find anywhere else, or that would be harder to find elsewhere. Knowing I've had those discoveries encourages me to keep using the Internet, to pop into it once in a while. But it still is inconsistent in coverage and quality; I wouldn't want to bet my job on finding information on the Internet.

## How do you start a research project? Do you normally go to the print sources first, or do you have a few online files or CD-ROM products that you always start with to get the lay of the land?

It could be any of those. I don't have a blueprint that's predictable in that sense. I first have to know who my requestor is. Even more important than what they're asking for, it helps to know who is asking the question, and what practice group they're with. I factor that in with what they're asking for and how much time I have. Money isn't usually a driving force—I'm going to try to be as economical as possible, but it's not something that really impacts where I would go.

## When you search the Internet, do you normally go to one of the search engines or do you have a list of favorite places that you go to directly?

I use a search engine when I can't remember what the exact URL is but I know enough to quickly find it through a search engine. But I generally don't turn to a search engine. I'll go to a specific site or a meta-site—a catalog of the best sites on a particular industry, for example.

## On the other end of the research, how do you know when to stop? What makes you decide that this is where you're going to pull the plug and wrap it up and send it to the client?

All the things I just mentioned play into that. Some of it is just instinct. I mean, you can always keep looking, but sometimes it's black and white. You know you've answered the question, period. For the questions that are gray, I'm sensitive to avoid overwhelming the requestor, because they're very busy, and we don't do a lot of packaging of information after a search. Obviously, we are making decisions about what we give people—we're not doing data dumps; we're a bit more picky and discriminating than that. But in many cases, particularly if they're hitting us early in the project, we send them abstracts or keywords in context rather than full text, so we can be more generous and broad in what we forward to them.

What I look for is whether I have given them enough information to get them headed in the direction that they need to go in order to get to a final decision. In many cases, when I send information to people, I know very well that this is not the final request for their project. So I send it in a format that's easy for them to browse. I send them examples or nuggets of information that will get them focused, stimulate their thinking, help them go through whatever process they have to go through to apply this information to their problem. And I always leave the door open, because in many cases I know that they will be coming back for more. Knowing when to end a search has to do with knowing my customer and understanding enough about information to know that answering the question doesn't necessarily mean an exhaustive search.

## You were on a panel at Online World called "The Way We Search Now." There was an interesting discussion among the panelists of whether or not we've become more casual searchers now, or whether we're still very structured in our research practices. Where do you fall in that continuum?

I think I'm somewhere in the middle. I was never very good at checking my Dialog Bluesheets, and I confess that in my entire career of searching Dialog I've never, ever used Dialindex. That sort of takes the fun out of it for me. But I wouldn't say that I'm sloppy; I just like to think as I'm going along. As you get more experienced using sources, whatever they are, you can to some extent create your strategy dynamically, get where you want to go as you're in the process of exploring it. So I probably veer a bit more toward the casual end of the continuum. I do like to chart things out a little bit in the beginning; I think that's my structure. In my environment I do have to be very conscious of time because we are charging our requestors, so I'd like to think that I'm not wasting time. And I don't have the time to waste, even if I wasn't charging them for it.

## What do you think it takes to be an expert business searcher?

To be a good searcher, you have to have a certain mindset. I'm not quite certain I know what that is, but obviously some people are better at being searchers and other people are better at other aspects of the information profession. In addition to being able to multitask and think fast on your feet, for me the trick of survival has been just keeping up—keeping up with the literature and going to conferences and letting yourself be constantly challenged by these things, not feeling threatened or frustrated. To hang loose and be willing to explore and have fun with it. More than anything, that's what has enabled me to survive as a searcher.

## How do you stay updated on new services and new features, learning that one of your favorite databases is now available in a new format or there's a new pricing structure?

I read everything. We subscribe to many newsletters, magazines and newspapers, and I read everything. I've made a commitment throughout my career to keep up with reading. I have also begun to subscribe to some email newsletters. I like *InfoAlert* [85] a lot. John MacDonnell, the editor, also edits an electronic newsletter called "Really Useful Business Sites," which is only available to *InfoAlert* subscribers. It's one of the very few things that comes regularly to my email account that I make a point of reading. I also like the *CyberSkeptic's Guide* [76]. For government information, the *Internet Connection* [90], and anything in *Online* [92] or *Database* [77] I gobble up. There are some industry-specific newsletters that we're starting to subscribe to as well. It's hard to find the time to keep up on all this reading; I do it mostly at home in the evening or on weekends.

## Do you subscribe to any electronic discussion groups?

I do not subscribe to very many; I find that they really eat up my time. I subscribe to SLA's Business & Finance Division's listserv [67], the SLA Legal Division's listserv [71] and the tax librarians' listserv [73]. I'm also a member of the American Association of Law Libraries, and I belong to their listserv [62]. One of the things I like about all those listservs is that the discussions seem to be more focused and more timely, as opposed to a forum for general conversation. It's not that there's anything wrong with a listserv like that, but that kind of forum isn't helpful for me.

I'm sure that if I had the time to keep up with a listserv like Buslib [63], I'd find lots and lots of wonderful nuggets. But I only have so much time in a day, and I just know that I wouldn't be able to manage it. So for those precious nuggets, I fall back on the magazines and newspapers and newsletters I subscribe to, and I stay in touch with my peers and pick up the phone and pick their brains.

## When you send the results of your research to a requestor, what format do they prefer?

We use Lotus Notes in my company, so most clients prefer that we send it to them electronically. We read them the riot act in the very beginning: We not only need their email address but we need their fax number and we need their mailing address, because sometimes the network's not available or it doesn't work when you try to load a file electronically. We still do crack books; I'm not afraid to disclose that. So sometimes it's a combination of materials that we have to get to them. But if we can send it electronically, that's their preference. We do not do a lot of fancy packaging in my library. We download stuff cleanly, we eliminate any search commands, and do a lot of cutting and pasting to make sure that we're sending them just the most relevant and useful information. We will work with Excel, too, if there's anything we're downloading that they want in a spreadsheet format.

# What do you like most about searching? What is it that keeps you doing this kind of work?

Partly, it is the detective aspect, getting your hands in the middle of something that's sticky and gooey, and molding it and creating something. It's not only finding the answer—although often that turns into a major part of the challenge—but discovering the nuances of the answer and the additional questions that come out of finding that answer. What do you do with those additional questions? Do you leave them alone because the person only asked for X? Or do you go ahead and bring in all the other stuff and muddy up the waters?

And I really love using information sources. There is something alluring for me in using the Internet. Every time you go somewhere, even if it's to a site that you've been to before, it's a new discovery. The Internet itself is still so new that every time I search it, I'm discovering how to use it. That's how it was for me years ago when I was first starting to learn Dialog.

## And what do you like least about searching?

When it starts to get very routine. It's funny; I don't think it would have occurred to me to feel this way six months or a year ago, but with all the changes going on with the professional online services, it's forced me to start looking at other sources. Quite honestly, the Internet has forced me to do that too, which is probably a healthy thing. I think searching Dialog has become boring.

## Is it boring because the sources haven't changed much and the search tools are pretty much the same as they have been, or do you just feel that you've explored its boundaries and now you're in back in charted waters again?

Probably all those reasons. Dialog is somewhat predictable in how you search it, and there haven't been a whole lot of new sources added. Perhaps it's even gotten a little boring to look at. Maybe we've been influenced by the use of images on the Internet. I'm very fortunate in my information center because I have a tremendous variety of formats and resources, and the Internet has opened up a whole new dimension. I may get to like the Internet.

## Where do you see the information profession heading in the next five years?

I've always felt that librarians were capable of doing lots of different things. What we call ourselves may change, and we may describe what we do in different words, but I don't see the profession as we know it going away. I think that there still will be librarians providing traditional services. They may not necessarily be in the environments that we've known, although I hope to some extent those won't go away. There still will be librarians who are generalists and who serve a large, diversified group. And there are going to be more and more librarians who support groups with very focused interests. And, yes, I think we will be Webmasters and involved with indexing on the Web. I see us doing more of what we're already doing, just doing it in different environments, across different platforms, maybe being called different names.

Even ten or twenty years ago there were librarians who were doing consulting work before that was the thing to do. And there were librarians who were knowledge managers before it was called that. There are always innovators and people who have more nontraditional and varied ways of defining roles. I think that that's going to continue to evolve.

# Super Searcher Power Tips

▶ The fun of the game is having to figure out which sources to use. You've got so many sources to choose from, and you have to determine which are the best ones.

▶ Knowing when a search is completed has to do with knowing my customer and understanding that the best answer doesn't necessarily mean an exhaustive search.

▶ As you get more experienced using sources, whatever they are, you can to some extent create your strategy dynamically, get where you want to go as you're in the process of exploring it.

# Tom Sterner

## Business Investigator

Tom Sterner is Associate Director of Investigations for Control Risks Group in New York. He has been using online databases in business investigations since 1987.

Tom.Sterner@control-risks.com
www.crg.com

## Tell me about your background and how you wound up doing online research.

I graduated from a liberal arts college with a degree in political science in the early '80s and worked as a paralegal in a law firm for a while. By chance, I got to know a partner in the firm because he used some of the paralegal staff to do online research for investigative projects. At the time, he had just started a private investigative company on the side; during the mid-eighties there was a lot of merger and acquisition activity, so there was a growing need for investigators. Eventually, he quit his law practice and devoted himself full time to this investigative firm. It grew and he needed people, and I joined the Investigative Group Inc. (IGI), as it was then known, as an online researcher.

So that's essentially how I got my start. I'm self-taught with online research. Actually, I had a mentor who was also self-taught, who established the accounts and the research department, as it were, at IGI. Together, he and I built the department over the years as the demand grew. But I had no formal training in online research; it was all sort of futzing around on databases, starting out with Lexis-Nexis [40, see Appendix A]. My big challenge, back in 1988, was

83

trying to figure out how to use Dialog [20]. I remembered seeing it in college; the reference library used Dialog but wouldn't allow anyone else to use it. Just like Lexis-Nexis, I learned how to use Dialog by on-the-job training, snooping around, trying to find new information sources.

## What kind of research do you focus on at Control Risks Group?

I mainly do business investigations, ranging from due diligence investigations to what we call litigation support and fraud investigations. I manage the various research aspects of all of these, which include a fair dose of online research, manual public records research in the field and, as appropriate, interviews. The interviews might be with former employees or with competitors and, depending on the nature of the investigation, they might be confrontational or not.

The litigation support investigations involve establishing the fact-pattern side of the lawsuit. Our task is to help prove or disprove certain facts being alleged, either by our client or by the opposition. That could be as simple as placing a certain person at a certain place at a certain time, or it might be establishing an undisclosed relationship between two people. It might be identifying past instances of inappropriate business activity by the opposing party, things of that nature. In some cases, it might be vetting an expert witness to determine whether or not they've been credible in the past or have been rebuked by a judge.

In most cases, particularly with the online stuff, the information I develop is included in a written or oral report to the client, combined with the other findings. Other colleagues of mine do strictly online research and might present that to me, or to another colleague who is also coordinating the other aspects of the investigation, acting as sort of a central repository. It's very rare that we present raw results of online searches to our clients. It's always in the context of other information, trying to address the specific client's issues.

# Can you walk me through a typical project?

Here's a typical scenario. We've been approached by a client who thinks that one or more employees might be involved with some self-dealings, some conflicts of interest. They've heard these rumors and they want us to try to determine whether there's something to them. The way we begin is to do a full-blown background check on these people, largely using databases. That will include trying to get every bit of information we can on them—where they live, where they've gone to school, what other businesses they're affiliated with, who they've borrowed money from, whether they've recently come into a great deal of money.

We rely very heavily on the public records databases. What we're trying to do there is find examples of vendors that have been favored by these employees, which might indicate that they are receiving kickbacks or something. So we scan the databases and look at possible leads. At that point, we might pull selected documents from the public record. For example, although in most states the online Secretary of State records list one or two officers or directors, the filings themselves often have more information—another address, a signature (that's relevant in cases of forgery), and so on. So we'll order selected documents or lawsuit filings and review those, and then, based on any leads we find there, do a second round of online research, and so on. We might go through two rounds of online public records research, put together the picture we have, and then begin to interview people.

# Is it the same iterative process when you're looking for information on a company as opposed to an individual?

The two aren't that dissimilar, at least in general process. The sources themselves are quite different, especially in the case of publicly owned companies. Privately held companies are the trickiest to research, of course. I have to say that, in my experience over the years, the richest vein of information on private companies has been litigation. Many researchers either don't think of it or don't have the budget to pursue it. For example, take a private company that does business in five different states. It's a relatively cheap search, a hundred bucks maybe, to search this company name or the affiliated companies in the Information America [33] Nationwide Lawsuit Index. And it's a pittance to search that name through the U.S. Party Index on Pacer [50]. So for a hundred and twenty bucks, you might be able to identify ten lawsuits involving this company, regardless of whether it's public or private.

We'd love to find allegations of fraud if that might be relevant to our investigation. But in most cases, what we're looking for are lawyers who've done the research, interviewed people, looked at documents during the discovery process, and laid out in court pleadings exactly where this company is, who its principals are, who its owners are, that sort of thing. The difficult part about it is that you can spend a lot of time and money looking at this kind of information and come up fairly thin. But there just are not many other sources, because companies don't have to disclose this stuff. Of course, if the company is in an industry that's required to file information with a federal or state agency, that's another source to try.

**A lot of people are turned off by public records because they look so dry and boring and dense. Some researchers just throw up their hands and say, "Oh, well, there must be a Dun & Bradstreet report I can use instead."**

I think that's right. War has been described as endless hours of boredom punctuated by a few minutes of terror. There's a similar process to reviewing court filings—you spend five hours bored to tears, and then you can stumble upon a document that breaks things wide open. Sometimes it will provide you with the exact clue you need to find additional information, or, if you're doing a due diligence search, the document may reveal something that the client specifically wants to know about.

Here's a great example that I always like to use: I was working for a lender who was in a dispute over a loan; the relationship went sour between my client and the other party. I went through six or eight boxes of court documents, trying to find whatever I could about this company and its borrowing relationships in the past. One of the boxes contained a huge lawsuit that really had nothing to do with any of the issues in my case. But it so happened that an exhibit attached to a pleading in this massive case was a draft complaint that had never been filed in the public record, that outlined a case very similar to my client's—a previous lender was making the very same allegations that my client was making. Attached to *that* was an internal document from the bank that specifically spoke to the behavior of certain people involved in the case. It was really a needle in a haystack, but when it was brought up in court, it caused my client's adversaries to settle, because they knew the judge was going to be very unsympathetic to somebody who engaged in the same practice over and over again, trying to stiff lenders. It was a perfect situation. If the party hadn't settled, we had the names of five people we could call to get even more details about the party's previous behavior.

# Have you noticed that having information available on the Internet has changed how you do research? Are you finding that more information from government filings is on the

## Net now, or do you still rely on the proprietary databases?

I still favor the commercial databases fairly heavily. I wrote an article about this in the *National Law Journal's* Law Technology Product News [www.ljx.com/ltpn/april98/sterner_p26.html] in which I made the argument that, in terms of content and convenience of access, the Internet just can't match the commercial databases, at least for public records. Of course, things are constantly changing. I used to have to pick up the phone to call the National Association of Securities Dealers to find out whether or not a broker-dealer had been disciplined; now I look it up on the Web site [43]. But I don't use any of the commercial services via the Web. The slowness of the connection absolutely maddens me.

On the other hand, I try to find stuff out on the Net that represents holes in what the commercial services offer. You know, figuring out whether FDIC information is more comprehensive on its Web site than it is in a Lexis-Nexis library, for example.

## How do you make those evaluations? Do you read the professional journals, or do you just spend some time noodling around in the site to see if it meets your needs?

It's mostly noodling, I have to say. I used to read the online trade journals more than I do now, and my searching efficiency has probably dropped because I'm not reading them as carefully. But I'm a huge proponent of the process of snooping around, because it allows you to do your own comparison rather than rely on someone else's judgment. When the time comes for you to decide which source to use, you can say, "I use this because I've compared it to this other source and I saw this advantage and that advantage." And my needs are going to be different than the next person's, so sometimes I'm looking for different things to compare.

# Which of the professional online services do you go to first? Which one do you consider your home system?

It depends entirely on the nature of the investigation. I often begin with a public records database like CDB [13], Information America, or Superior Information Services [57], which focuses on the Eastern U.S. They're useful if I need to get, for example, a history of where a person has lived over the past ten years. But in terms of company information, business affiliations, press reports, stock trades, things like that, Dialog is my favorite source.

On the Net, I use companies' Web sites, although I don't rely on them. In some cases, company Web sites have a great deal more information than a Dun & Bradstreet report. In some cases, they have more than news reports, especially for private companies. Usually, I use Web sites for leads—to verify addresses or to compare phone numbers to see if there might be an errant phone number that's been used by the company. And sometimes I use a company's Web site as a starting point, to see how they describe themselves.

I make fairly heavy use of the big search engines like AltaVista [2] and HotBot [31], just to cast the net wide and see what comes up. For example, there have been a number of cases in which I've found a person affiliated with a company, which they did not disclose on their curriculum vitae. This is useful when we're working with investors who want background checks into the principals of a company they're about to invest in. I might find an affiliation that they've never heard of, which obviously raises questions as to why it wasn't disclosed. I worked on a fraud case involving alleged theft of intellectual property. I found one of the parties representing *another* company on a European trade conference site on the Net. I guess he just figured that nobody would ever put the two together. You absolutely never know what little tidbit is going to be out there if you look.

Privacy is obviously a huge concern in this kind of research. We're very aware of the privacy issues; there's a lot of legislation now that's intended to limit access to the most sensitive personal information. In this day and age, unless you proactively attempt to maintain your obscurity, privacy is quickly diminishing. But when you think about it, we're just using different methods to try to get at the same information. One can do more at one's desktop than one used to be able to, but the privacy issues are really not that different from what they were fifty years ago.

## Since you make use of a lot of the fee-based services, how do you select the most cost-effective source?

We constantly try to be efficient in our searching. By efficient I mean, first of all, knowing how to use search engines cost-effectively, and second, knowing content—not going online and doing a public records search when three out of four counties' records you're searching are not even covered in the database. Our clients will often do that—go into Information America and do a search and find nothing, and wonder why. There's no *there* there, that's why they didn't find anything. Perhaps the counties they were searching weren't included in the database. It's a constant struggle that I've found no consistent solution to after doing this for ten years—knowing which is the best source for each particular investigation. I just try to maintain the efficiencies as much as I can.

I think that fixed-price contracts can be very favorable, although I've seen ones from some vendors that are very unfavorable to the subscriber. The big problem is that you get an all-you-can-eat value, and then you gorge, and when it comes time to recalculating the price next year, it's based on your inefficiency in searching. On the other hand, as investigators, fixed-price contracts are very valuable to us because they really allow you to sniff down various leads and not worry about the cost. You want to be able to follow every scent, and if it dies off, then just come back and pick up the next one.

## How do you make those judgment calls about which source to use when the same material is available on several online services, a CD-ROM, and maybe directly from the vendor?

Those decisions are almost entirely driven by content. I don't find myself doing a tremendous amount of budgeting. Let me give you an example. Let's say I'm investigating ten people in New York, and I want to know what lawsuits have been filed in New York. If there is essentially equal content on two providers, I'll take the next step and assess where I can realize the benefits. In some cases, the benefits might be purely cost; i.e., I can string together these ten searches for a flat fee and not pay print charges, as opposed to paying per name. Additionally, though, I'll wonder whether one of the search engines will allow me to manipulate that data in ways that another might not. For example, the full-text search engine capability and the Focus feature on Nexis are tremendously useful when you retrieve a big set and then just want to play around with that set—looking at different relationships, whether it be ZIP codes or last names or all companies with the name "Zip" in it, or various oddities like that.

In another case, though, I know I can use CDB Infotek to search a tremendous number of public records in California for a flat fee that I'm not going to exceed even if I find four hundred records. If I do that same search in the California Records file in Lexis-Nexis, for example, I'm going to run up a much higher bill. But I'm not going to have as much content as I do on CDB. Then again, I would like to do that same search in Lexis-Nexis for the flexibility of playing around with the searches. So it really depends. If I'm working on a fraud case, chances are I'm going to use something that will allow me the flexibility to do some real snooping around with a large set. If it's a due diligence case, I might be more interested in coverage that's as broad as I can get, to make sure that if this guy has a DUI in Alameda County I can pick that up, as well as identify another corporation that he has somewhere else in California.

## It's an amazing calculation that we wind up doing—it's almost subconscious.

That's right. A lot of this is sort of embedded knowledge, if you will.

## How do you decide when you've found enough information to stop? Do you usually know that what you've found is all that's available, or do you just get to the point where you know that it won't be cost-effective to find anything more?

I would say the latter. Some cases are very straightforward, where you make sure that you've covered the relevant press databases and the relevant public records databases, and for a certain budget that's what you've agreed to do. But there are a number of projects where we're just beginning to develop leads on cases and it's difficult to know when to stop—the connection might be with this company and not with that company. What I try to do in those cases is calculate what the budget is going to involve and what databases we'll need to search, and let the client know that this is what is going to be covered. But chances are we're going to develop leads in one source that then need to be followed up somewhere else. We generally try to approach it in phases. Clients are receptive to this approach, both conceptually and for budgetary reasons. "Let's see what turns up in phase one" is a common response among our clients. They assume that we'll at least pick up the obvious information at the beginning.

It's a challenge, though, to decide what resources to use with that first-phase budget. You don't have enough money to do searches in five jurisdictions, for example; you can only do three. You choose the three that you think are most likely to give you the information you need, but in some cases you might only find that felony fraud conviction in the fifth jurisdiction. If you've been in this business long enough, certain patterns occur and certain leads smell richer than others, but you can never be entirely sure. So the phase one/phase two approach can be problematic. But I'd say on balance it's a workable model, both for developing information and working with a budget that is amenable to the client.

We're always very clear with a client as to what we've searched and what we haven't. We'll explain, for example, that the local newspaper in the town where this person has lived and worked for the last five years is not online. So if the client wanted to find out whether there are any reported incidents of problems with the company that the individual ran, we would need to send somebody to the local library or the newspaper archive to do manual searches. That's how we protect both ourselves and our client, in terms of knowing exactly where they stand and how thorough the search has been.

There are instances where the client has a very specific question and you can answer that question with a fairly high degree of reliability halfway through your budget, so that's when you stop. But that's the exception rather than the rule; the rule is we cover A through D on the first phase, write up our report, then tell the client that, based upon what we found, we recommend searching these other jurisdictions or these other company names.

**One of the hardest parts of being a researcher is knowing in the back of your mind all the places that you *could* go if you had unlimited time and budget, and then figuring out the**

# places that are likely to give you the biggest bang for the buck.

That's true, especially since the clients are beginning to think that databases are miraculous—you just need to punch in a name and it comes back with the answer. The Internet has raised clients' expectations about what we can do, and also lowered their appreciation of how hard it can be to actually do it. If there is no other good reason to cover Internet resources for a project, you do it anyway, to avoid the situation in which you give your report to your client and the client says, "By the way, I found this on the Internet as I was watching TV. Did you find that?" They learn to appreciate your skills and the difficulty of Internet research, though, when you report to them five important items that they *didn't* find after spending three hours on the Internet.

# What is the most fun part of searching? What is it that keeps you doing this kind of work?

I find myself continually challenged by puzzling out exactly what is available through databases and what's not. It's a notion that I harp on, but I really enjoy knowing what is in these databases. I shiver at the notion of people walking up to a terminal and punching in a name and thinking they've covered all the bases. To me, really understanding how search engines work, how content is gathered, how it's updated, how it's purged—I find all of that quite interesting. Large portions of the user population just don't have any idea about any of that, and when I talk with vendors about these sorts of things, I find that even a lot of the customer support people have no idea what they're supporting. They don't understand what goes into the gathering of the data, what its potential value is to a certain type of client, what might be more valuable to a certain customer base, or what search feature might improve things. I guess it's just an odd little bit of the world that

I, unlike most people, have come to understand. You know, there's something perversely thrilling about knowing something that many other people don't understand.

## And what do you like least about online searching?

Well, there are things that tick me off and things I really don't like—and they aren't necessarily the same. What frustrates me is dealing with customer service people who don't understand their product. I realize that they don't use some of these systems as much as I do, so they've not gone through the trial and error process that I have. All I ask is that they recognize that, and be responsive to queries. When I ask a question about content and I hear somebody say, "Oh, it *should* be on there." Well, either it is or it isn't. There's no "should" about it. If you're not sure, please go find out. It's zeros and ones, basically, and I can't go back to my client and say, "Well, I *think* that criminal records from Los Angeles County were covered."

I get very hot under the collar when vendors don't treat my concerns with interest. I remember a time when I discovered just by chance that the Pennsylvania real estate file in Nexis contained no Erie County data. There was not a single record from Erie County in that file, simply because of an error in updating the database. We're talking tens of thousands of records that were not included, and potentially hundreds of queries that were made, and nobody had any idea of the problem. They just did the search and it was a null set or they found five records in other counties but none in Erie County; how were they to know that it was an incomplete search? I knew that this person owned land in Erie County, though, so I recognized the problem. I remember getting into a long discussion with the head public records person at Lexis-Nexis about it. "Don't you feel any obligation to disclose to your customers that there hasn't been an update, that they've been searching a null set? Isn't there sort of a, for the lack of a better term, *moral obligation* here from an information perspective?" That sort of thing really ticks me off.

What I like least about online searching is that there's a certain tedium to using some of these sources over and over and over again. But there are probably lots of jobs out there in the world that are a lot more tedious. The boring projects just come with the territory; they're sometimes the bread and butter part of our business.

# Where do you think the information profession is headed? Where do you think we're going to be in five years?

I'm bullish on the profession if for no other reason than information overload. I think the way the curve goes is that people start to get excited: "Oh, we can do this," and then they begin to realize, "Wow, this takes a lot of time, and I don't really think I know what I'm doing." With the growth of information comes that much more demand for specialization in the information industry. Knowing exactly how to use systems, knowing exactly what is on each system, feeling very comfortable about the research I've done—that's going to become much more important once everyone becomes completely overwhelmed by the world of information and the search process itself.

We're seeing a lot of providers trying for the supermarket approach of providing something for everybody. I prefer to use a system that does not try to appeal to the lowest common denominator. My biggest concern is about content. I've been in this business for ten years, and I've seen some really great sources of information get dropped by information providers simply because they weren't getting enough use. I'm concerned, as an information professional, that the vendors will become even more willing to drop files that haven't been accessed X times a month when they start marketing to a broader base.

My other concern is the quality of vendors coming into the market. There is a company that has entered the online public records market within the last couple of years; I see a tremendous number of people using this company, and relying pretty heavily on what it offers in terms of online information. Some esteemed colleagues and I have found, when we've scratched the surface, some pretty severe examples of unreliability of the company's data. I'm very concerned that a company like that can generate a huge amount of revenue in a short period of time because people aren't asking questions and information professionals aren't evaluating it as carefully as they should. Ultimately, it makes my job harder because I need to scrutinize each new entrant a little more carefully and be a little more suspect about it.

I find that people have gotten into this business who don't really understand the information industry. They just see the opportunity to make money; they treat it like any other business, and they don't really know how to respond to some of the concerns. It's not a commodity, like selling orange juice—it's a more subtle, sophisticated product.

# Super Searcher Power Tips

▶ It's very rare that we present raw results of online searches to our clients. It's always in the context of other information, trying to address their specific issues.

▶ In my experience over the years, the richest vein of information on private companies has been litigation.

▶ In terms of content and convenience of access, the Internet just can't match the commercial databases.

▶ If there is no other good reason to cover Internet resources for a project, you do it anyway, to avoid the situation in which you give your report to your client and the client says, "By the way, I found this on the Internet as I was watching TV. Did you find that?"

# Grace Villamora
## Ad Industry Info Pro

Grace Villamora is president of Wesearch Worldwide, Inc., based in Chicago. Her company focuses on providing business research and library consultancy to the advertising industry.

**wsearchw@ix.netcom.com**

## Tell me a little about your background and how you started your business.

I've always been in advertising, even when I lived in Manila; I was in the creative aspect of the ad agency business. I graduated with a degree in public administration, and then I moved to Chicago and went back into the advertising industry. Eventually I was given an opportunity at Ogilvy & Mather to set up an information center. I enrolled in several library courses that were recommended by SLA, and I set up Ogilvy's library from scratch. It was a business and visual library because I was servicing account executives, media people and the creative staff. I started the library in an empty room with one desk and two phones, and when I left Ogilvy & Mather we had 10,000 titles. I introduced online searching; at the time the library was set up, we just had an acoustic coupler, a PC and a Lexis-Nexis [40, see Appendix A] UBIQ terminal. Eventually we moved on to using Dow Jones [21] and other online services.

After I had been at Ogilvy for eight years, I was offered a job to start another ad agency library at Tatham, Laird and Kudner, now Euro RSCG Tatham. I took that job and set up an information center there. I introduced online searching and established a creative library where the art directors and copywriters could come to uti-lize images and background information for storyboards and cre-ative campaigns.

I stayed there for three years, and then I was offered a job at DDB Needham to reorganize their information center. So I moved there and came in as Director of the Information Center, reporting to the senior vice president of strategic planning and research. After eleven months, they gave me a promotion to vice president. I didn't ask for it; I just worked like a storm because I liked the environment.

At that agency, I created a really special creative library. It was a dedicated room for creative research, and we had all kinds of pic-ture files and art books. We utilized the Dover and Bettmann Archives for indexing, designed with the needs of the creative pro-fessionals in mind. The creative guys would come in and ask for pictures of people playing football, people playing soccer, people ballroom-dancing, pictures of rock and roll artists, nature, houses, a picture of a hammer that was sold by Sears in 1945, you name it! We had song books because music is a very powerful component in commercials, especially if you're big on TV. Sometimes people would come in and sing to us, and want us to look for the lyrics of a song they were humming. It was fun!

I was very active in the new-business committee; I would sit in on the meetings when we would identify and map out what prod-uct or client to pitch for. In my job, I was an entrepreneur for the agency. I introduced a current awareness service through the information center, and I sold the service to Discover Card, Maybelline and Walt Disney. Walt Disney was not even a client of the agency; they were a client of the information center directly. I packaged the current awareness reports so that each one looked like a customized newsletter, and clients received it on the third working day of each month. It was a different newsletter for each client, depending on their business and what they requested. If they wanted us to monitor a competitor or a new market, then we would do a current awareness search on that subject. I relied on the PROMT files on Dialog [20] for most of the searches.

When the president of DDB Needham in New York retired, he opened his own business and he called me for information. The same thing happened when other executives of the company left to open their own businesses—they would call me for research work. Eventually, we began charging them, and my department was showing a profit. At that point I began to say, "Gee whiz, I could be doing this on my own!" At one point, I was practically working seven days a week and I thought, "Oh my God, I made a mistake. I introduced too much! I can't hire enough people, but I have to continue doing this work because my clients are expecting this service." That's when I decided that maybe I'd be okay doing it on my own because I had established a lot of contacts with people in ad agencies.

There are also a lot of freelancers in ad agencies. Even if someone is employed full-time, once in a while they're given a fantastic offer and they work weekends and nights and they produce something. And they'd call me for research help. So that's how I got started with my own business in 1993.

Then I discovered AIIP [74] through Stan Moreo, another independent information professional in Chicago. At one point I'd said, "Do I really like doing this?" I felt so isolated and I just had to talk to someone else who was in the same setting, who was also starting up his own business. Stan Moreo was wonderful; he told me, "You *must* join AIIP," so I went to my first AIIP conference, and here I am, all these years later.

I decided to start focusing more on the international market because, at the time, the economies of Asia and Eastern Europe were really strong, thriving and full of hope. Being an Asian, I know how to work with Asian businessmen and could tap into my old network. I used to work in ad agencies when I was in Manila, and I would go to Hong Kong, I'd go to Sydney, I'd go to Singapore.

# Can you describe a typical online research project?

The thing about my research is that I've been in the industry for a long time. While some projects are new, a lot have that feeling of déjà vu. I know intuitively what sources to use, because I've done the same kind of search before. The other thing about my clients is that they are in communications, so they're always in a hurry.

One example of a typical project was when a client called and said, "In two days we're going to meet with a potential client. We've got to know the candle market very quickly—aromatic candles, holiday candles. We'd like to know who's buying them, we want to know sales figures, we want to know the distribution channels." Fortunately, I remembered that when I had done research on the greeting card market, I would always see candles positioned near greeting cards. I also remembered reading in *Discount Merchandiser* that greeting cards are often sold in discount stores. That prompted me to try a quick search in IAC InSite [32], with a focus on discount stores. I found twenty-five articles, looked through them and found several that discussed the marketing of candles. I noted that the product code for candles was 3999400 so I did a second search using that product code. I found some very useful articles, especially one article that gave me almost everything—an industry overview, sales information, distribution channels, pricing, marketing and promotion strategies, consumer demographics and candle industry facts. I also followed the links that InSite includes to companies featured in the article and other related concepts.

Then I used my print copy of the *Encyclopedia of Associations* [78] and found the National Candle Association, in Washington, DC. Usually when I call an association, I try to talk with the director or the executive research manager, whoever handles research. When I got in touch with the head of research at the National Candle Association, I asked for any industry reports they might have produced. He said "No, we don't have anything like that, but we can fax you our publication *Candle Facts*." OK, I was willing to settle for that. Unfortunately, most of what they faxed wasn't useful to me, because it talked about how you can collect candles and put them in old-fashioned jars, and about safety tips regarding candles. There was a discussion of candles for every occasion, which answered one of my client's questions about what kinds of candles are available.

Then I decided to go on the Internet because the association maintains a Web site at www.candles.org. As it turns out, they have a lot of information there that they didn't tell me about over the phone! From the Web site, I found that U.S. consumer candle retail sales are currently $2 billion annually, and the industry is growing at the rate of ten to fifteen percent annually. Candles are sold principally in three types of retail outlets—department stores, gift shops and mass merchandisers. So there you go with the distribution channel question. As for seasonal sales, thirty-five percent of their sales are during the Christmas holidays and sixty-five percent is nonseasonal business. The Web site also indicated that there are two thousand varieties of candles and that women are the main purchasers of candles. It also covered current trends, product extensions like aromatherapy, and all kinds of fragrances. I was able to get all this information very quickly, in less than an hour. My client had called me at 10:00 in the morning and said, "How about getting it to me some time tomorrow afternoon?" So I waited for the next afternoon to send the material!

**If you pull a rabbit out of a hat too often, the clients start expecting miracles every time. In general, are you using the Net more**

## than you used to for research or using it to find sources you wouldn't find otherwise?

No, not really. I had a very large project recently in which the client didn't want me to use the Net, just commercial databases. He wanted me to look for reviews of books used in executive seminars. He wanted to identify books on topics like corporate image, employee involvement, employee motivation, product development. And he needed the initial report in ten days. I knew that I could get reviews online from *Harvard Business Review*, *Sloan Management Review* and *Across the Board*. I also looked through my back issues of *Business Week*, *Forbes*, and *Fortune* because they're a lot easier to use in print than in the online versions. I also used some academic management journals, and found enough for my initial report. For the second portion of the research, he said, "Just give me ten sites on the Internet that might have some book reviews." That was very tough; I thought, "I should have started with the Internet right away." But how would I have known at the beginning that he'd ask for this after the first part of the project was delivered?

Sometimes I *will* start on the Internet because I know the information is there—I've seen it. For example, if I'm looking for market research reports on telecommunications or health care, I would go to Frost and Sullivan's Web site [27]. I can get executive summaries, and sometimes that's enough for the client.

## When you are using the Net for research, how do you search efficiently?

I subscribe to Danny Sullivan's Search Engine Watch [65], and I read it and tag things I'd like to check out because they're new. I also have a bookmark file of search engines that I arrange according to topics. When I don't really know what to do and where to go, I use that first. I want to use the Net, but most of the time I'm in a hurry, and I trust the commercial databases more than the Internet.

Of course, I'm talking here about the free sources on the Net; I use the Web-based versions of Dow Jones [21] and Dialog. On the other hand, the processing of the information kills me. I've tried using the Web-based versions of the commercial databases, but then I go back to the old way, the traditional way of searching. I can get the information, put it into a Word document, and have very little garbage to delete. It's much easier to clean up output from the dial-up version of an online service than it is from the Web version.

But, more and more, I have been asked to develop Web bibliographies for clients. One client asked me to create profiles of a number of telecommunications companies, and he also wanted me to go on the Web and tag the good Web sites and give him a list. For clients like that, I usually send my report electronically, so they can manipulate the data if they need to.

## How do you deal with the issues of reliability and retrievability of information you find on the Web? What about the question of figuring out who really owns a site or who's responsible for the information?

I think that's the reason why, more and more, I'm delivering Web bibliographies and encouraging clients to download and evaluate the information from the sites themselves. I think about copyright issues too. Most of my clients are either presidents or senior vice presidents and they're not afraid to go onto the Web—mainly because I came in and trained them on the Net already! I teach clients how to use the Net, and then they understand that it's not easy to search the Internet. I know I'll never hear them say, "You can't find anything? I'll find it on the Net for you."

## So you don't often hear clients say, "I've already looked on the Web, and I know that

# there's nothing there," or "Why don't you just do a Web search? I know that this won't cost much because everything's on the Web and it's all free."

I don't hear the latter, no. What I hear is more like "I have searched for this and can't find anything; can you help me?" They call me because they know that I can find it. It took a while to develop this strategic business practice. Two or three years ago, people were saying, "Go on the Web, it's free, it's easy, everything's there." So whenever I would come in for a client presentation, I would always give a live Internet presentation. I would ask them to search for something and then I would search the same thing and give them an example of how I did it. I would show them what they missed and what I missed (and I always prayed that what I missed was not a lot). Giving a live demonstration of the wild world of the Web is great, especially in advertising, where they're always in a hurry. They see that it's such a slow process, even if you have a T-1 line. It's not the speed of the connection as much as it is the inherent lag of Net searching that slows things down.

# What professional online services do you rely on?

I have subscriptions to Dialog, Dow Jones, Nexis [40], IAC InSite, and Manning & Napier [41], and I use them all. And of course whenever any new commercial database offers a free trial, I take it. Then, if it's something I think clients should have access to, I make sure they subscribe; they pay for it, but I search it for them. I know that they have better things to do than maintain search skills on all these databases. I'm trying to introduce them to some online skills, but strategically. My clients don't search every day because they have other things to do with their time. They're paying for the subscription, and they can always use it when they're in a jam on the weekend, for example.

I also go to database update sessions whenever I can and pass the information along to clients. I know they usually won't have time to try it, but I do it because we have an open relationship, an alliance.

## How do you stay up on top of news about enhancements to databases and about new services coming down the pike?

I go to professional conferences like Online World. And I get news through listservs, and every day I do business reading. This is a habit I acquired when I was in the ad agencies; I would read advertising columns, marketing columns, investment columns. Now I read them electronically—*The Washington Post*, *The New York Times*, *The Wall Street Journal*, *Los Angeles Times*—every morning, after I've checked my horoscope. I always check my horoscope first; who knows ... it might tell me "Today, you will lose your memory! Check your computer!"

In terms of listservs, I subscribe to AIIP-L [61], the SLA listservs for the Consultants section [69], and the Information Technology [70], Communications [68], and Advertising [66] divisions. And of course I read Buslib [63]. Every day just for fun I also go to www.suck.com for the lighter side of things. Also, a client of mine has me monitoring what Yahoo! and some of the other search engines are doing with their banners, so I do that as well.

## So you wind up looking at the parts of a Web site that I never look at; I try to ignore the ads!

That's my perspective because of the clients I have. That's also the reason why, in addition to reading the newspapers electronically, I have to read them in hard copy when I have time. I have to read at least *The Wall Street Journal*, *The New York Times* and *The Chicago Tribune* in print format to see how the ads are positioned. People forget sometimes that the electronic version of the paper eliminates the content and the nuances of ad placement. I'm looking at content in several different ways. When I look at a Web site, I look not only at the text but also at the banners and placement of ads.

I'm also paying attention to audio clips. Sometimes I need to monitor music from radio broadcasts in Brazil or South Africa because a client needs South African music or Brazilian songs. It's a lot of work to find, but it's fun to be able to monitor music from anywhere in the world. Searching is very different now because we have more resources to use—we couldn't monitor Brazilian radio broadcasts before the Web!—but it requires a lot of time. I have to exercise due diligence, and it involves a lot of consulting with my clients, explaining that this is a new site and it may work or it may not, and it may disappear next week. But they like to push the envelope, so I provide them with the sites.

I have a client who is in public affairs/public relations, and more and more they want to listen to radio interviews. The Internet is wonderful for them; not only do they have access to radio broadcasts, but they also can scan electronic discussions with Deja News [19]. Sometimes my job is just to discover an electronic discussion group or a chat group that they can monitor themselves. They will tell me that they have a prospective client and they need to stay on top of what's being said, so that they can react immediately if need be. It's almost like being able to monitor a focus group.

## Do you use the Net much for international information, or do you find that most of that

## information is still only available on the professional online services?

In my experience, much of the information isn't available online anywhere. When I had a number of Asian clients, I often needed market research, position papers, papers I purchased from think tanks. The only commercial database I used for international clients was Dun & Bradstreet [22]. Now, much of that information may be available on the Internet.

The other factor we tend to forget is that our telecommunications system is far superior to most countries', the problem with my Asian clients was access. Sure, they have the Internet, but the telecommunications system is not good, so they can't access what we can as quickly. That's the reason why many international clients use us—the instability of the telecom infrastructure—plus they don't know where to go to find the information they're looking for. Several times when I was in Asia, I would try to access what I would easily get to here in Chicago, but I couldn't get a connection. Or there was a typhoon and so we lost power. I kept thinking, "Let me get into the American Embassy and I can access it right away!"

## But you can't just set up shop in the embassy, can you? When you're doing a search, how do you know when to stop? Sometimes you simply run out of time with these short turn- around projects, but what about when you have enough time to explore the options?

I know that I've gotten most of the good stuff because I've answered most of the client's questions. Also, I always have a budget cap. I've talked to a client and we've agreed on X amount of time and money, and when we hit that point, I'll stop. But even then, I'll always give it one or two extra hours. That's the way I am, and I think most professionals do this too; that's the way you keep clients. You cannot really measure your hours and your seconds, and besides, it all averages out.

I know when to stop because my budget or my time has run out. But even then, as soon as I finish the project, I usually set up a current awareness profile with Newspage [46] and similar free Internet sites on the topic I just searched. So the next day, if there's a relevant article on the topic I just researched I would get it into email. I would give it to the client as a value-added service, and I would say, "Oh, by the way, my deadline is over, but my current awareness is still on and I found this information." They appreciate it.

## How do you decide when to use a source on the Internet and when to use one of the commercial online services?

I still believe at this point that the best way to meet a client's research need is through a commercial database. It's well-indexed, there are standards, and it's reliable. The Internet is an added value I can offer when I have time, unless clients say, "I just want the Internet because I don't want to spend a lot. Just give me something to get me going, and I will get back to you if I need more." Mainly, I use the commercial databases because most of the information I retrieve is for business development, or it's a competitive monitor, and I still don't have one-hundred-percent faith in what I get from the Internet. I spend time double-checking things; when I prepare a Web bibliography, I always add in parentheses the date searched so that they'll have a reference time, and will understand that it might not be there when they search it in six months.

That issue comes up when I give client presentations too. I will give a canned demonstration of Net searching and show some sites, but I always have a disclaimer to the effect that I developed this presentation months ago so when you go back to your offices this might not be there. But still, when I get ready for a demo, I wake up at 5:00 in the morning and search to make sure the spot is still there for my 9:00 appointment!

Most of the time I don't do live demos. I just use canned presentations. It's exciting, it's in color, and it's also controlled, so I know I won't hit any dead sites during my demo.

## What do you like most about online searching?

I like it because as I keep searching I learn more, and as I learn more it's easier to search. I like sitting down and doing my search strategy, keeping in mind that, even though I use my personal resource directory, there might still be something new, given time and budget, that I can do for clients. I never really get the same question twice. That's why I don't save my search strategies, because the information environment will be different the next time I do a search.

## What frustrates you most about online research?

The slowness of the process. What also frustrates me sometimes is when I see records that are misindexed, words that are misspelled, because then you have to go back to the document and correct it before you send it to the client. I know that the database was probably created in Greece or China where they're just transcribing what they see, but they don't necessarily notice mistakes in punctuation or spelling. That means that *I* have to clean up the typos and formatting errors. But I still like research—when I'm working on a big project for a client, I do more than online searching: I interview, I visit stores if I have time, I do manual research. There is still a lot that is not online or on the Internet.

## Where do you think the information profession is heading? Some people believe that, with the

## rise of the Internet, everybody's going to be doing their own searching and we information professionals will face a dire future. What's your take on all that?

*Au contraire!* I think we have a huge opportunity to grow. I think that we as information professionals—assuming that we have the basic competencies—will play a pivotal role. Clients cannot quickly realign their skills or acquire new skills in order to keep up with the technological changes, but we can. So we'll play a critical role in the knowledge industry as we acquire greater depth, flexibility and focus on what we do uniquely well. We'll be able to undertake more projects, clients will give up doing it on their own because they'll realize that they're getting the wrong information or that they're spending a lot of time.

## I am always surprised when a client calls and tells me, "I spent six hours on the Net and couldn't find anything. Can you help?" I always wonder how they found all that free time to waste looking for information.

Well, some people just have the time. I got a call from somebody from Rancho Mirage, California. She told me that she needed someone to do a search for her. She asked me if I could find the name of an Italian tenor who performed at the Lyric Opera. The opera was *Il Trovatore* and the performance was a matinee in 1935. Apparently it was her favorite performance, and she wanted a review of the performance and information on the tenor.

As it turns out, she called me just before Thanksgiving, so I was in a very good mood, and I thought "My God, I'm going to the microfilm files and look for this thing for her." I found it and I was so thrilled.

# Do you have any hints or keys to your success as an information professional?

Those who will survive are those who really enjoy doing research, and when you enjoy doing it, you think of your clients more and more. For example, you read what they're reading. You join groups that they're active in. You do *pro bono* work together. That only enhances your business and your reputation. It's really a matter of building alliances, being part of a team with your clients. For example, I introduce my clients to Dialog and Dow Jones, and I arrange for workshops to be conducted in clients' offices. It's a sharing environment. They know that we are the experts, that they should come to us for industrial-strength research because they don't have time. It isn't threatening to our profession to teach our clients about how we do research.

Sometimes you have to be creative in your research, you have to think outside of the box. A lot of times it is intuitive, like that candle project; I was already aware that candles are often displayed near greeting cards. I try to look at the world from my client's perspective, because that's how you are able to communicate well. That's how, even if you're not physically with clients, you are a team, and they will always think about you first.

One time I was in the elevator in my office building, and I had all four clients who also work in the building in the elevator with me, and they were peppering me with questions! In fact, one client didn't get off at her floor; she followed me to my floor and when I went to the washroom, she followed me, saying, "Maybe you can answer a question ..." Just seeing people face to face sometimes gets me a new project. Last month I was walking along Michigan Avenue and I ran into a client who said, "I have a project for you!"

Running my own business, I still sometimes deal with the issue of isolation and not seeing enough people face to face, even though I have an office outside my home. It's probably because I used to work in an ad agency and you'd hear people fighting and shouting and screaming and having fun! Or coming to the office when it's Pajama Day and everyone is in pajamas. These days, of course, I can work in my own library in pajamas whenever I want!

# Super Searcher Power Tips

► I want to use the Net, but most of the time I'm in a hurry and I trust the commercial databases more than the Internet.

► Those who will survive are those who really enjoy doing research, and when you enjoy doing it, you think of your clients more and more.

► You have to be creative in your research, you have to think outside of the box. I try to look at the world from my client's perspective, because that's how you are able to communicate well.

► As soon as I finish the project, I set up a current awareness profile on the subject on several free Internet sites and forward any relevant articles to my client, as a value-added service.

# Bob Berkman
## Author and Editor

Robert Berkman is the Editor of *The Information Advisor*, published by Find/SVP and, at the time of this interview, was Executive Editor, Internet and Lifestyles at Ziff-Davis Journals (Rochester, NY).

rberkman@aol.com

## To start, tell me a little bit about your background and how you wound up where you are today.

My first real job out of college was as an editor at McGraw-Hill in New York City with a new information service product for local governments called the Product Information Network. One of my primary jobs was to write articles and reports on all sorts of topics that would be of interest to local governments; it was kind of a *Consumer Reports* service for local governments. We might write a report on, say, how to buy a police cruiser, or tips on sanitation truck usage—things that cities would need to know.

Then people started asking me, "How do you learn about a new topic? You start off knowing nothing about it and then end up writing a report on the subject." And I found that people were intrigued about the research process by which you begin with no background on a topic, and then build enough knowledge to create a report. So I thought, "Hmm, maybe I'll develop a course on this for the Learning Annex," which provides adult education in New York City. They approved it, so I started teaching this course, How To Be an

Instant Expert on Any Subject, but it was really a course on how to use the library and conduct research.

This was back in 1981, so it was before a lot of online stuff was available. A few people who took the class said, "Hey, this would make an interesting book." At that time the Learning Annex had an agent who was turning some of its courses into books, so I contacted her. Eventually, someone from HarperCollins sat in on my class, liked it, and encouraged me to write a book proposal. That became the book that was published in 1987 and is now in its fourth edition, called *Find It Fast: How to Uncover Expert Information on Any Subject* [80, see Appendix A].

I'm kind of glad that I didn't have any training in library science because if I did, I don't think I would have been able to write that book. I didn't know about information science and sources. I would have been too overwhelmed to think that I could write a book on this topic. Ignorance was bliss. I started from scratch, thinking, "This will make an interesting topic for a book," not knowing that librarians and information specialists have all these journals and guidebooks on finding information. I just based the book on things that I learned on my own.

So that led me to the whole research area. When I moved to Rochester, New York, I got a job at a market research company called the Winters Group as the director of secondary research. That's where I really started focusing on doing business research for clients, but I found that I missed publishing. So in 1987, I decided I'd start up a newsletter for some Winters Group clients and other people who do market research. I called some clients and said, "What are your biggest problems with finding information?" A lot of them said, "Assessing the quality of information. There's so much out there, how do you know what's any good?" So I came up with this newsletter called *The Information Advisor* [86], which would be a consumer's guide to information sources for business researchers. I took the newsletter with me when I left the Winters

Group a couple years later, and I've been editing it for more than ten years now. It was purchased by Find/SVP in 1993.

I learned the information field from a journalist/outsider perspective, as opposed to being trained as a librarian or a searcher. But I became intimately familiar with the needs and problems of that group from having been the editor of the newsletter and from being immersed in the field. I've written some other books, *Find It Online* [81], and a number of books for Find/SVP, including *Finding Business Research on the Web* [82], and I'm working on a book now for NYU Press on academic research. One thing has led to the next: Research led to online searching, which led to business online searching. I still do online research, although I now have an official day-to-day office job at Ziff-Davis managing and developing new Internet-related newsletters.

## How do you decide how to begin a search when you want to get smart on a new topic?

I try to think about who would care about this topic. Asking the right question compels the answer, so cultivating the art of asking good questions is a way to cut through the fog of information overload. Of course, knowing how to ask good questions means being familiar with your industry so you know the key questions to ask.

After a while, knowing what kind of source to use is mostly intuition. These days, the two sources I toggle back and forth between are Dialog [20] and the Internet. I like going to Dialog if I want very focused, summarized, rich, filtered data, especially from trade journals. I know I can get the voice of an expert who's analyzed the phenomenon. I call it dense information—it's tight, concise; it's gone through the traditional editing process.

One of the newsletters I'm in charge of here at Ziff-Davis is about online investing, so I needed to get up to speed quickly on that whole topic. I wanted a really focused summary of the issues, so I went to the trade journals on Dialog to find out the hot issues, what people are talking about, what the experts say are some of the problems of online investing. I've developed sort of a template for my business research on Dialog: I do a OneSearch of five or six of my favorite files, and then eliminate duplicates. Files 9, 15, 148, 275, 16 and 636 *[Editor's note: Business & Industry, ABI/Inform, IAC Trade & Industry Database, IAC Computer Database, IAC PROMT and IAC Newsletter Database]* are my standard OneSearch business research starting points. The other databases I use a lot are newspaper databases and the company directory files.

I'll go to the Web when I want the opposite type of information—raw data, just a fact, or something that's obscure or unusual, something that doesn't necessarily have to be filtered through any process.

# I like your description of Dialog as containing "dense information." If fifty percent of your Dialog search results are irrelevant, you think you've done a very unfocused search, whereas if half of the hits from a Web search are useful, you think you've hit the jackpot. Speaking of which, when you search the Net, where do you usually start?

Ninety-five percent of the time I'll start at AltaVista [2], because I know it the best; I know how to use all its features, I know its quirks. I still like the fact that you can use the NEAR operator, though I've been doing less and less of that. I used to always use the advanced search feature, because I assumed that's where you could do the most sophisticated, precise searching. But as time has gone by, I find that I prefer the simple search option, but using the same search features that are available on the advanced search screen. I make sure I know how to use the pluses and minuses, the quotation marks, truncation, and title and

URL searching. If I know how to construct a really good search with the right fields and extra search features, then I'll use Alta-Vista's simple search option.

## How do you handle the situation where you try a search and retrieve far more information than you can possibly absorb?

I have my own way of focusing a search and avoiding being over-loaded with information, especially if it's a topic that I think will have a lot written about it. I'll often limit a search to some specific journals that I like a lot, like *Fortune* magazine or *The Economist*. I'm pre-screening via an assumption that if an article is in that jour-nal it'll have useful insights. If I need to focus even more narrowly, sometimes I'll even limit the search to a particular person. Maybe I'll just want to see what Barbara Quint has written about a topic, or Marydee Ojala.

I think one of the keys to coping with information overload is finding out your most trusted sources on a specific topic. Obviously, the drawback is that you're limiting the scope of what you're going to retrieve, but when you think you're going to be swamped with information, you want the best analysis. So you think about where you're most likely to get it, what has proven to be your favorite jour-nal, and then just search that source or that author.

## So that lets you build a broader search, by making the universe you're searching very small.

Exactly. For example, recently I had to do research on how pub-lishers can market via the Internet. I thought, "What journals do I like that might cover this question, from a perspective that's useful for me?" I limited my search to two journals that I liked and trust-ed and that seemed most relevant—the American Marketing

Association's *Marketing News* and *Folio*. It's a matter of thinking on a really narrow level, so you can limit your search by knowing which journals are best to zero in on.

## It's a case of knowing your sources, too; being familiar enough with an industry to know that a reliable source for publishing information is *Folio*, for example.

The more you know about the industry, the better your searching is going to be. And of course, knowing an online service well makes you a better searcher too.

I find that the nice thing about getting familiar with one or two of the professional online services is that I have a general sense of how big the universe is there. I know that if I do a search and get X number of hits, I can be pretty sure that I've gotten most of what's out there, whereas when I'm searching an online service I don't know well or a file that I'm not familiar with, I can never quite tell if I've retrieved most of the good stuff or not. I don't think that sense of assurance ever really comes with the Internet, because the universe is constantly expanding.

## Have you found that you search differently, now that there are different kinds of information available on the Internet? What things are you looking for now that you couldn't find a few years ago?

I'm very intrigued with the concept of anecdotal information on the Web. Obviously there are questions about reliability and quality of information. But now, for the first time, there is this massive amount of personal experience available at the push of a button. For example, I've done some searches for friends or relatives who had medical questions, and often they said that it was helpful just finding out what to expect from someone else who has gone through a certain operation.

Tapping in to people and their experiences is really a new source of knowledge—at least in the sense that it's searchable now. And whether it's recommendations on a product or a company, or the kinds of issues people talk about in their day-to-day lives, I think this is the biggest kind of new information on the Internet.

I had an interesting example a few months ago. My cat had a seizure, so I did a quick search on the Web. I went to AltaVista and typed +cat* +seizure*, and found a great Web site. It was built by a graduate student whose cat had had a seizure, and who then did extensive research on why it happened and what to do about it, and found links to veterinarians who specialize in it. It was a very comprehensive site, and it was the kind of information that, without the Net, I never would have found. Tapping into people who have some experience that can be of direct benefit to you makes the Net most intriguing.

## I know that you tap into librarians' discussion groups when you're working on an article for *The Information Advisor*.

Oh, yes. From an editor's viewpoint, listservs are fantastic tools, because you're always looking for case studies and anecdotes. For example, if I'm reviewing a new product for *Information Advisor*, I could call the vendor and say, "Can I have some references?" But you know you're only going to be referred to people who are happy with the vendor's product. It's not exactly a representative sample of users. But I can go out to the targeted group of people who are likely to have used that product and ask, "Hey, can someone tell me what your experiences are with using this product?" Then I get a much fairer, less biased sample. I have had tremendous success getting helpful comments from people on Buslib [63], the business librarians' listserv, who have said, "Yes, I tried this and I liked X, Y and Z about it, but I didn't like this or that." Again, that is something that would have been extremely difficult, if not impossible, to do effectively before the Internet. Even though the number of people on listservs has grown exponentially, listservs are still serving their purpose, enabling people to share ideas and information. I still think that, in some ways, electronic discussion lists are the best part of the Internet as a whole—certainly for business researchers.

## It's hard to keep up with new information sources and new features of information services. I read periodicals like *The Information Advisor*, but what do you, as *IA* editor, do? How do you stay on top of everything, since you're supposed to be two steps ahead of us?

That's a scary thought! Well, I keep up with professional reading. I don't get to it nearly as much as I should—it's the whole information overload question. But I try to read *Online* [92], *Database* [77], *Searcher* [94] and *Information Today* [88]. I like *Information World Review* [89] a lot, and recently I've been enjoying *Brill's Content* [75] magazine as well.

But also, I find it really helpful to stay on the Buslib listserv to see what's on people's minds, what their problems are, what they're grappling with, what's the hot topic people are talking about. If I see something that's causing some debate or some concern, I'll look into it as a potential topic for *The Information Advisor*. And, of course, I go to the conferences like Online World and National Online to see if a vendor has something significantly new and potentially useful that's going to solve a problem.

The key is knowing as intimately as possible what the issues and problems of my readers are, staying on top of what they're doing. The

Buslib listserv is a great way to do that. I also do reader surveys occasionally, and I get good feedback from readers about the things that are causing them problems and some of the issues that they're dealing with.

## Do you subscribe to any electronic newsletters?

The only thing I get regularly in email is Search Engine Watch [65] by Danny Sullivan. I find that really valuable for staying on top of developments specifically related to search engines. But I generally find that I like *less* coming at me. I'm very judicious with that. I'd rather think through what I want to find, and then search out that specific piece of information or that expert, rather than be buried with lots of stuff and then sort through it. That means asking the right questions in order to find the information that answers my own specific needs.

## One thing that I've noticed over the last few years is that the same information is sold through a number of channels. What does all that mean to business searchers?

It definitely makes things trickier in some ways; when you have more choices, you have to spend time figuring out your best choice. That's one of the missions of *The Information Advisor*—to look at a database that's available on, say, three professional online services, the Net, a CD-ROM, and two niche Net sites, and then compare what you can do and what the features and costs are for each.

Definitely, it takes time and effort for somebody to hunt down these different sources and compare them and see what's available, because everyone's trying to leverage their strength with another medium or another vendor. In some ways it's better for the user because you do have these additional outlets and other places you can search, and maybe you'll find something that's better, but that's predicated on (1) knowing all the places where the product is available and (2) knowing how they compare. That's very time-consuming; you almost have to dedicate someone in your organization full-time to research the alternatives.

I walked into a supermarket a couple of months ago to buy a toothbrush and there were eight million different types: rounded, shaped, short bristles, long bristles, antibacterial, this and that. All I wanted was a toothbrush! I was staring at that display, mesmerized by the number of choices. That's the thing; we're definitely in the age of over-choice.

There's an optimum level of choice, but a lot of it is not necessarily driven by the searchers or the consumers. It's driven by the vendors, who are concentrating on putting a lot out there, trying to find different niche markets, trying to attract different audiences. That just makes things more confusing, ultimately. It's one of the results of a free market—on the one hand, you get lots of choices, but on the other, you've got to *deal* with all those choices.

**Related to that is the time-versus-money trade-off. You can access a database through one of the end-user services for very little cost, but there's often a trade-off in terms of both search power and system responsiveness. On the other hand, there are some features such as the search result folders on Northern Light that you don't get when searching the same files on Dialog or Lexis-Nexis. How do you make those calls about which service to search?**

I'm lucky because I can get a press pass for Dialog. I can go onto Dialog and feel quite blessed. I really like searching, so it's like somebody who loves food and is given a free pass to the best restaurant in New York City—you just go in and gorge yourself and don't pay anything.

My big problem with searching databases on the Web is that, while it's convenient, I'm really annoyed by the time it takes to click through pages and wait for downloads. I sometimes search Dialog Classic through the Web because it's convenient, since I'm already in my browser. But it's still so much slower. I'm used to systems being instantaneous. Waiting for the Web can be frustrating when you're searching a professional database.

**I think that's especially the case when you're searching Dialog and you're used to watching a clock. You watch the minutes tick by as a page loads and loads and loads. Argh!**

Exactly. I've become accustomed to real-time, instantaneous responses, so three to five seconds of waiting seems interminable now. Part of it is that we're living in an age where instantaneousness has become the norm. I'm not sure how healthy that is in terms of day-to-day quality of life. When I go home after searching, I find that I'm less patient with somebody who takes a minute to get to the point of what they're saying, or who's struggling with the right word. You get used to operating at the speed of the microprocessor.

**Yes, we do. On a different topic, what do you do when you've got a research project that's tough to identify? Say you hear about an issue on an electronic discussion group but you're not sure how to articulate it in enough**

## detail to research it. Or when you simply aren't sure where to start your research?

Sometimes I do some general searches and get leads on what the key issues are. Then I go back and rethink and rephrase my question. It's sort of a backwards process, but it works: doing research to find out what you should be researching.

When I'm not sure where to start, I may just hop on the Web. It's free, and it's easy to get on a search engine, type in a couple of words and see what comes up.

One thing to keep in mind is that, for certain types of information, it's not really necessary to search the professional online services. Press releases, for example. You don't have to go to PR Newswire or BusinessWire on Dialog. Breaking news items and press releases have now become a commodity and are available for free on the Web. News has become the free giveaway, in a sense, to attract people to a Web site.

## Are there other types of information that you used to search for on the professional online services that you now get from the Net?

Recent news, press releases, and basic company directory facts are all on the Web for free, whether it's at Hoover's [30] or one of the other sources like CorpTech [18]. You can get to some fairly extensive information sources, like sites that have industry ratios and data on companies. Straightforward facts from a company's PR office you can definitely get directly from the Web. But analysis is still in short supply on the Web—investigative reports that you'd only read in a really good print journal, or a good analysis that you might find in a market research report—though these are migrating to the Web now, too.

There's going to be more and more analytical information available because everything's moving to the Web. It's not likely to be free, but I have a feeling that the general price pressure of the Web, meaning that everything should be free or nearly free, will make those $3,000 market research reports available in much less expensive, bite-size chunks. I'm still debating whether those expensive in-depth Wall Street reports are going to become more commodity-like as well, or whether they will retain their high pricing. I'm not sure where that's going to fall out. But I do know that anything that goes through the Web faces definite price pressures, and chances are there will be downward price pressures on the analytical information that's still in short supply on the Web.

One nice thing is that these market research firms will often provide excerpts or abstracts of some of their reports on their Web sites, so you may find a piece of information that you wanted—a statistic or a market shipment date or whatever—that you would have had to pay for in the past.

Publishers are still grappling with the question of what to do with the Net, and few of them have really found a successful model yet. They're all trying; they feel they have to be out there on the Web. But it's still such an unknown, and no one really has *the* answer as to what publishers need to be doing to successfully market on the Web. It makes for interesting times.

## We are definitely living in interesting times. Tell me, what do you enjoy most about searching?

I like the intellectual challenge—I know the information's out there; now, how do I find it? The other thing I like is finding something that I wasn't sure would be there, some really obscure piece of information. For example, one time I was trying to track down the title of an old 33-1/3 LP from the late 1950s or early '60s that my brother and I used to listen to as kids before we went to sleep at night. It was a story about a bear who was mistaken for a construction worker, called "The Bear That Wasn't." I think my mother had accidentally thrown it away, and we were always saying, "Oh, why did she ever throw that away?" Old record stores would search their databases and could never find it. I would regularly check flea markets and garage sales, but never found it. So I heard about this listserv called Stumpers [72] and posted my question on it. Sure enough, someone pointed me to the Bowling Green University Library of Popular Culture [10], which has a huge collection of popular culture audio archives. So I called them, and sure enough, they searched their files for that title and found it, and recorded the LP onto a cassette tape—all for four dollars. I gave my brother this tape as a present. He couldn't believe that I had actually found it, twenty-five years later. That's the kind of fun stuff I like about searching, being amazed when you actually find some really obscure piece of information.

## How have you dealt with reliability of information on the Web? When it's not clear who's putting the information out there, how do you gauge the trustworthiness of a site?

It's a difficult thing, because now everybody can be a publisher. What the Web is missing that traditional media have is someone picking up the role of editor. The reader or searcher has to step into the role of editor. If I find information from an individual's Web page, I'll send an email message with a couple of follow-up questions, and then see how that person replies. I can get a sense from the reply if the person seems responsive and knowledgeable.

Ultimately, it comes down to using your gut to tell you if the information sounds right. But there are specific things that you can do: Confirm it with a second source and ask follow-up questions. Journalists have standard ways of evaluating a source: Who is this person, what is his background, what are his credentials, what is his organization, what is the mission of that organization?

You know how you trust your next-door neighbor to your left rather than your neighbor to the right when you ask for a recommendation for someone to fix the roof. It's more complicated when you've got an unknown entity on the Web; it's a lot harder to develop that trust. I'm grateful that all this information's out there, and my experience has been that most sources have been very helpful. Someone will have a passionate interest in the topic, and they're out there because they want to share it with everyone else. But contacting the person and talking to them, either by phone or email, is a good way to fill out your sense of how much this person really knows.

Of course, it's a lot easier to assess the quality of someone else's information if you already know something about the topic yourself. If you don't, you can always run that person's information by some- one you *do* know who is familiar with the topic. To go back to the example I gave of finding information on cat seizures on the Web, I could have printed out the Web site and brought it to my veterinarian and asked, "Does this make sense?"

## It sounds like everybody needs to use journalists' skills now in evaluating sources on the Web.

The good thing about the Internet is that it does allow all these voices that, for better or worse, are not represented in the main- stream media. You have access to people with fringe opinions, which in some cases might mean the lunatics, but in other cases could mean people who just are ahead of everybody else or have a slightly different point of view that's not being represented. You have more choices, but you have to take on the job of ferreting it out and determining its validity yourself.

## Where do you think the information professional's future is heading?

There's no question that people will continue to do more and more of their own searching. That's where the vendors are concentrating their new products—having people doing more of their own searching, for better or worse. I have a feeling that we'll continue to see businesspeople doing their own searching, at least for facts and for data. But I also think that it is very confusing and difficult to do a good job at this, and that's where the business information professional could take on the role of trainer.

One area of opportunity for information professionals is in knowledge management. Organizations want to make strategic use of their internal and external data, and there are many examples now of business information professionals who are key players on the team, if not the leaders—Ellyn Knapp at Coopers & Lybrand, for example. Knowledge management goes through phases; it has its ups and downs. But the ability to tap into an organization's information and leverage it for strategic advantage is an issue that's not going to go away. And if it remains an issue, then the trained information professional clearly should be playing a key role.

The other issue that's not going away is information overload. We'll see more and more searchable databases on the Web, and a lot of these sites are going to have no quality control or consistency. It's the role of the information professional to start establishing standards and quality control.

In general, we're seeing a lot of changes in the information environment, and that's especially hard for mid-career information professionals who began their careers before the Internet. A lot of them thought that searching would always be in the domain of professional searchers and not the hoi polloi. All of a sudden they're seeing their area of expertise being co-opted by the general public and trying to figure out where their role is now. That can be a little disheartening, unless they look at the new opportunities available at the intersection of information technology and business. If anybody can expand their role at this point, it's information professionals.

# Super Searcher Power Tips

▶ Asking the right question compels the answer, so cultivating the art of asking good questions is a way to cut through the fog of information overload.

▶ I go to the professional online services when I need very focused, summarized, rich, filtered data—what I call "dense information." I go to the Web when I want raw data, just a fact, or something that's obscure or unusual.

▶ I often limit a search to some specific journals that I like a lot. I'm pre-screening via an assumption that if an article is in that journal it'll have useful insights.

▶ I use the Net if I need to find recent news, press releases, basic company directory facts—even fairly extensive information on companies. But analysis is still in short supply on the Web.

▶ What the Web is missing and that traditional media have is someone picking up the role of editor. Ultimately, it comes down to using your gut to tell you if the information sounds right.

# Elizabeth Swan
## Information Professional Down Under

Elizabeth Swan is the owner of Information Edge Pty. Ltd. in Sydney, Australia. This interview was conducted via email over the course of several weeks. What follows is an edited transcript of the email interview.

**infoedge@ozemail.com.au**
**www.information-edge.com/~infoedge**

## Tell me something about your background and how you came to start your own business.

After graduating from the University of Queensland, I became a "reluctant" librarian at a provincial university in Australia, largely because I couldn't find anything else to do with a history major. Then I moved to the Architecture School at the University of Melbourne, where I started to discover and enjoy research librarianship, as opposed to custodial librarianship.

While intermittently traveling around Europe for nearly four years, I was fortunate to have a number of special-library jobs in the U.K. I returned to Europe, and I was very fortunate to be employed in 1971 by Dr. Pierre Vinken, then director of Excerpta Medica, and later Chairman of the Elsevier group. I learned about marketing and about electronic databases, how Embase was created, the differences between Embase and Medlars, and the relationship between the printed products and the databases. I will always treasure the time spent at Excerpta Medica. I learned so much from Pierre and his team.

Back in Australia, I tried not to work as a librarian again—but was offered the job as manager of a large industrial library for

Australian Consolidated Industries (ACI) Ltd., one of Australia's leading listed companies at the time.

Initially, I found it difficult to be enthusiastic about beer bottles and bottle tops and some of the other products the company manufactured, but the job proved to be both demanding and interesting. We introduced Dialog [20, see Appendix A] and Orbit [52] to the company late in 1975. Shortly after that, we also subscribed to Textline. When affordable pricing was introduced, we subscribed to Ausinet [7], which was operated by ACI's computing arm. Our library databases—citations and abstracts of journal articles, company technical reports, company market research reports, and the library catalogue—were private databases on Ausinet.

Eventually, we were undertaking strategic searches supporting mergers and acquisitions activities and, in 1987, the protection of ACI from a hostile takeover. But in 1988, the hostile takeover succeeded and, along with thousands of other staff, we were made redundant with the throwaway line "Can you find a university to take you over so we can still use you?"

We collected our redundancy payments and attended outplacement consulting. I bought the company database of journal articles and accepted the offer of then-State Librarian Alison Crook to form a joint venture with the State Library of New South Wales to be called Information Edge Pty. Ltd. Information Edge would be an information broker and database producer, and my equity in the company was the corporate database I had bought from ACI, from which we produced current awareness bulletins for ACI staff. I also received a government grant of A$20,000 to assist with the planning of the venture and the relationship with the State Library. The company was launched in 1989 with the Library Council of New South Wales owning fifty-percent equity; I owned the remaining fifty percent.

The concept of a joint venture between a Statutory Authority and a sole woman created a lot of interest and we received considerable publicity. ACI personnel continued to be customers, but we also built up a sizable customer base as a result of that publicity.

In 1996, I had an opportunity to buy the State Library's equity, so the company is now one-hundred-percent privately owned. With a full-time staff of four and additional part-time staff, we operate from offices in the heart of Sydney.

# Tell me about your job. What kind of business research do you do, and who are your main clients?

Primarily, we provide research to solve problems for our clients in business and in government. We have several hundred customers—many in Australia and New Zealand, and some farther afield. We are strong online searchers, but we do manual searches when necessary. We also seek information from experts in the field. Sometimes the only way to solve a problem is to scan through old magazines, files, indexes or even archives. On other occasions, the spoken word is more useful than the written word.

We also provide document-supply services for articles that aren't available in full text online. And we produce the Edge database, now on Dow Jones [21] and Informit Online [35], and from this we produce newsletters. *Management Edge* summarizes a selection of current management articles that we believe are informative and useful. *Packaging Edge* summarizes packaging and end-user product articles. *Building Edge* summarizes articles in some building product areas matching our clients' interests.

We also do some consulting in areas relating to special libraries. And with Maree Enright, a former ACI information scientist and now a professional trainer, we hold training courses on Tips and Tactics for Successful Searching.

# What do you look for when you're hiring a new researcher?

Finding good researchers is a challenge. There are some key characteristics we look for. They need to be intelligent; there are a lot of issues to come to terms with when using a wide variety of hosts and other sources, and we do research on a huge variety of topics. They need to be curious; if one is not interested in the topic of a search, it is hard to do a good job. They need to be literate; having a good vocabulary is a big advantage. They need to be good at algebra; how can one analyze and combine concepts successfully without this sort of mind? They need to like people; searchers are diminished if they cannot empathize with their clients. They need to be imaginative, or lateral-thinking; where and why would some information be published in *that* source? If we cannot find that Spanish article in Spanish, what about finding the same press release in an English-language newsletter, for example. They need to be persistent, but realistic. Persistence means they do not give up in five minutes when the required answer isn't immediately forthcoming. Realism comes into play when determining what a particular job is worth. And they need to be confident and flexible, willing to change tack if initial results are not promising, and able to handle new technology.

# Can you describe a typical research project?

A management consultant had been asked to review Department of Immigration activities at Sydney Airport and needed insights into the occupational health and safety aspects of shift work, and ideas on training Customs people. Another client, a Sydney solicitor, sought press articles from newspapers in Israel, the U.S. and Australia as evidence for a client who was a victim of the Maccabiah Bridge disaster outside Tel Aviv. A firm that develops heavy vehicle testing systems used by road transport authorities sought data on the relationship between rolling resistance and fuel consumption, and evidence of criminal proceedings resulting from trucks with defective brakes. They used the information we found for a marketing campaign.

## Tell me a little more about the Edge database that's on Dow Jones Interactive and Informit.

The Edge database was formerly ACI's private in-house database, produced so that company executives in about ten countries could be easily alerted to new, relevant information published in Australian and international journals.

Our focus was and still is on reporting articles that describe better ways to manage—to reduce costs, increase sales, reduce waste, improve performance and succeed in the marketplace. So there is a bias toward practical articles that contain information that can be implemented fairly easily. In recent years we have also added material relevant to government enterprises.

It is not as comprehensive as ABI/Inform, for instance, which I regard as one of the best management databases worldwide. Nor does it contain the full text of articles. We write abstracts to indicate content rather than try to reduce content to one paragraph. It seems rather unfashionable these days to produce a database of abstracts. But somehow I think that when everyone is so busy, there is still a place for a selection of summarized material for those who do not have time to read everything relevant, but who still want to be aware of key issues being addressed in reputable journals.

When I acquired the database from ACI in 1988, my dream was to turn it into an Australian version of the old Predicasts PROMT database, and to produce by-products from the database as Predicasts formerly did. This I have not yet been able to achieve fully. The management abstracts are also incorporated in the Business Australia OnDisc CD-ROM, and the entire database will shortly be on Informit Online and is already on Dow Jones.

# How do you decide where to begin a search? Do you usually start with, say, Yahoo! on the Net, or do you begin with Dialog or Dow Jones, or some other source?

I usually approach a search by thinking about where and why and when would someone publish the information I require. This helps me to choose whether I should use newspapers, scientific publications, corporate publications, articles that started life as press releases, and so on.

If the subject of a search matches the scope of our own database, I start there because I am so familiar with it and how to get the best out of it. It is great to use Edge for management topics, for instance, even if I later supplement the search with a search of other, bigger, more comprehensive sources. Likewise for information on, say, the beer industry in Australia; I know I will get lots of clues from the Edge database. Then I can move on to other sources to supplement where necessary.

If I am looking for information about products, these days I would check our Kompass [39] CD-ROM and then go to the Net, because companies are increasingly using the Net to promote their products. If my Net search results were not successful, I would look in trade journals or a source that indexes trade journals, or in an index of trade catalogues.

If I am looking for information that I think some government department, or some other organization with a charter to make its information freely available, would produce, again I would go to the Net. I like using AltaVista [2] because I can control precision fairly well. Sometimes, I may use Northern Light [47] or the Australian search engine Anzwers [5]. I now have a long list of organized bookmarks with some of my favorite sites.

If I am looking for scientific, refereed international information, I go almost immediately to a range of scientific databases. That is where I find Dialog's Dialindex so helpful. I choose a variety of categories and get a feel for where the volume of data is. This makes me aware of some files I would not normally use.

We have had a couple of spectacular successes using Dialindex. I am also a great fan of Dialog's OneSearch, or the facility in any service that allows me to search files concurrently and remove the duplicates easily. They are such powerful time-saving devices. A few years ago someone wanted to find out what type of concrete was used in the wharves at the Port of Singapore. By using the Allscience category in Dialindex, we found one reference; two Port of Singapore engineers had given a paper in English at a conference in Beijing describing the new wharves, and the Pascal database had indexed the conference papers. Who would have imagined that you would find the reference to a Singapore issue in a Parisian science database? A quick check in Australian Bibliographic Network [8] found that only one Australian library had a copy of the proceedings, and they faxed us a copy of the paper.

More recently, I was asked to locate a conference paper on a topic by an unknown author who possibly worked for one of two companies, maybe somewhere in the Northern Hemisphere, and gave a conference paper in the U.S., maybe in 1997. It was very satisfying to locate the 1996 paper quickly using Dialindex and then to confirm that it was the right one when we got a copy of the article from a library 1,500 miles away.

For Australian scientific or refereed information, the range of databases available is much smaller. Sometimes we will find the Australian information in the international files. For some specific topics we have good local databases. Streamline [56] is excellent for water research, Cinch [15] is excellent for criminology, and Family [26] is a very good local database for issues relating to families.

For local business information, we would often use Reuters Business Briefings [53] because it has comprehensive coverage of Australian newspapers for ninety days and we pay a flat fee per month, so the temptation is to get value for our money. But for more in-depth research farther back than ninety days, we use Dow Jones because it has the longest archive of Australian newspaper material. And certainly for searches that require complex search strategies we would use Dow Jones, as I find the search engine for Reuters better suited to searching for simple concepts like company names. I do not use the Internet versions of the Australian newspapers because it just is not convenient to search each newspaper one by one, and I am not confident I can rely on the Internet files to be complete or extensive enough for most of my needs—and their search engines are still fairly primitive.

## How has the availability of information on the Net changed how you do research? How has your searching changed over the past three or four years?

I cannot claim to have been an early user of the Internet for searching. I found its anarchic nature, its relatively weak search engines, and the slow response speed here in Australia totally frustrating. "Free" is not free to me, nor to my clients, if we fail to find needed information or if it takes hours to complete a task.

When I use any information resource, it is not to explore how it works or how it is indexed, it is to find information that may be crucial to a client, and that is nearly always needed quickly. Many of my peers in Australia were *au fait* with Internet searching long before I was, but I suspect they had the luxury of experimenting with the technology rather than using it to meet very specific information needs on tight deadlines.

However, the search engines are getting better and better. Access speeds seem to be better, connections more reliable, and I am now much more comfortable with it and have a much better grasp of when to use the Net and when to avoid it. I love being able to get government information quickly. It is very good for some company research, and in Australia we have a couple of very good legal sites where we can obtain case reports and/or statutory information. So it is great to be able to do a search, say, on a company to provide background for an executive search firm and then say, "Please note the reference to a court case—here is the Web site where the full case report can be found."

Has searching itself changed? Yes and no. Although we do a lot of online searches, we do quite a few manual searches too. It is surprising how often it is necessary to use old newspaper indexes, clipping files or even archives to locate information for court cases of one kind or another. Sometimes we write detailed summaries of the key facts contained in a search or after speaking with relevant experts. Company profiles may be brief or, if they are for competitive intelligence purposes, may be very thorough. The end product has to match the needs of our clients.

On the other hand, the Internet has brought to our desktops lots of resources not previously available conveniently—government information, promotional literature, some of the legal material we need in Australia, and so on. We are compiling reports that contain information from a greater variety of sources, and sometimes our reports contain referrals to Internet sites.

Except for the national bibliographic database Kinetica [38], we use library catalogues much less than we used to. Perhaps one reason is that major Australian libraries are scattered over a huge continent and therefore access is frequently difficult. Nor have we tried to use international library catalogues because ultimately we are seeking contents, not citations. Instead, we are compiling our own "Knowledge Index," which records where we found particularly useful information. It is a composite record of Internet sites, unusual databases, associations, consultants, libraries and other sources. In this way I hope we can economically and professionally keep track of the best sources for our clients.

## Do you have any flat-fee contracts with online vendors? If so, how do you handle charging your clients for usage?

Yes, we have a flat-fee contract with Reuters and now for Informit Online also. With Informit we were able to choose the databases to which we believe we will need access. I am assuming that if we get a job in a field for which we have not purchased access to the relevant database in advance, then we can simply buy access in a hurry and factor the costs into the quote for the job. We have also just negotiated a flat fee for Kinetica, which is an important resource for us.

I can understand why the vendors want to introduce this charging model, but it is difficult for information brokers to charge out costs when they are incurred as flat-fee contracts. And I am not at all surprised that the new Dialog is edging its way in that direction, because, from my experience, flat-fee contracts certainly do force up usage.

We can search *The Australian*, for instance—a major national newspaper—on either Presscom [51] or, now, on Reuters. As long as Reuters has sufficient archival data, and as long as the search is not too complicated, we use Reuters because of the flat-fee contract; we see it as a "sunk cost." Equally, we could use either Dow Jones or Reuters for material from the *Sydney Morning Herald* or the *Australian Financial Review* for material from the past ninety days. Again, we would use Reuters because of the sunk cost and because Reuters has a facility to let us know how many hours we have used each month. Dow Jones also has flat-fee pricing, but so far we have not been provided with any useful usage statistics.

How do we charge for flat-fee pricing? We calculate what it would cost us per minute and charge on a per-minute basis. To do that, though, you have to have a pretty good idea of how much time you will actually spend on the system. It is not good enough to divide the monthly contract by the number of minutes or even by the number of working minutes in a month!

# Lots of databases are available on a number of sources—on the professional online services, on the Net, through end-user interfaces like Dialog Web's Guided Search, on CD-ROM, and so on. How do you decide which one to use?

I sometimes wonder if I am like an old dog that is difficult to teach new tricks! Despite the recent proliferation of new ways of searching various databases, I have not migrated to new platforms to any great extent.

I like to use services that are reliable, fast, current, cost-effective, comprehensive, and where I don't have to remember lots of different passwords and IDs. I like search engines that allow me to seek out data with a scalpel rather than craft scissors and that allow me some freedom to explore. I think it is fair to pay for data if you can assess its relevance, but I think it is unfair to pay top price just to look. This list almost certainly disqualifies many CD-ROMs, as they are not current, fast or comprehensive enough for my needs.

This list also generally excludes alternative access methods for some databases available on the Net, because fiddling around from one site to another, searching databases one by one, each with a different password, is very slow and chews up time I cannot spare on behalf of my clients.

This list also favors the professional online services because they are generally very reliable, fast, current, comprehensive, and they have powerful search engines. I like being able to click on an icon and get into a service without the tedious process of password checking. My choice of service, though, may change if pricing options become too unfavorable. It's a question of trading off time against costs in order to achieve the best result.

## How do you stay updated on new information sources, new services, and new features? Do you subscribe to electronic discussion groups? Read magazines? Go to professional conferences?

We have only recently started getting into listservs. I quite enjoy reading the AIIP listserv [61] most of the time because its members are frequently dealing with issues that we deal with here. I am a little fearful of how much time listservs may waste, however.

We subscribe to *Database* [77], *Online* [92], *Information World Review* [89], *Information Outlook* [87] and *Online Currents* [93]. I have always read Dialog's *Chronolog* religiously and in the past considered it a benchmark for vendors' newsletters. I don't enjoy the Dialog email updates as much. They are probably cheaper to produce but they don't seem to be as informative—or is it just the difference between an email and a printed page?

Because of our database activities we also subscribe to international management journals. I find the material in the management literature about knowledge management or business intelligence, for instance, very enlightening.

I am a member of the Information Science Section Committee of the Australian Library and Information Association, which runs the Information Online and On Disc conference in Australia. Working on professional committees is a great way to keep up to date and to meet local and international leaders in the field.

In 1998, we also started the InfoEdge After5 Club for information professional colleagues. Once a month we invite a speaker from the information industry to talk to the club over a glass of champagne and a snack between 5:30 and 7:00 p.m. It's a very *laissez-faire* club—no registration, no officers, no rules—but everyone seems to enjoy it. Our first speaker was Derek Smith from Dialog, shortly after M.A.I.D. took over Dialog. Since then we have had speakers from Lexis-Nexis, Datastream, Dow Jones, the National Library of Australia, Reuters and other services, and we are booked up quite a few months ahead. It's an interesting forum. In such a small group we can get to ask some pertinent questions!

# What do you do when you don't know where to begin a search? Say it's in an area you're not familiar with, or a really general topic?

As part of the initial interview I try to get as much background information as I can. Usually I find clients are willing to share with me what projects they are working on. Sometimes it can be difficult and can take some time. I may have to do some quick research on the Net or in a reference book or in one of the databases we use to get an idea of the concepts involved. Thesauri, too, can be useful aids to navigate around unfamiliar topics.

Then I may phone the client back and say, "I wondered if I could just check on a couple of points to make sure I am on the right track." Our training partner, Maree Enright, calls this type of interviewing "using Columbo softeners" after the famous American television detective.

Asking "Why is the information needed?" is often difficult, as it appears to be attacking the client; asking for "some background information" is easier. Behind general questions, the client always has specific objectives. When the objective of a search is identified, starting it becomes easier.

For some searches, I may even make some suggestions about what is practical: "We may not be able to find XYZ, but we probably could find ABC; would this be useful?"

# How do you know when to end a search? When is enough enough?

We have two disciplines that help us know when to end a search. Firstly, we define the objectives—what are we aiming at, over what time period, in what languages, in what countries, theoretical or practical, thorough or a few key references, etc. If you have defined objectives, it is easier to know when to end a search. Of course, in the process, we may come across other issues that may need to be addressed, and these we report in our key point summaries. Then the client has the option of pursuing the other issues as a next phase, if necessary.

The second discipline is that we frequently work under budgets. We have some clients who simply want us to do the best possible job, and budgets are not discussed. They are experienced clients comfortable with our charging process. To reduce new clients' anxiety about possible costs, we recommend budgets within which we can work. This is not easy for us to do because it is so hard to predict costs and how long individual jobs will take, but it is a discipline we try to adopt. When there is a budget, it is easy to determine when "enough is enough"—it is when you reach the budget limit!

# Any other searching tips you'd like to pass along?

Good business information research frequently calls for lots of tenacity and plenty of lateral thinking. It also requires more intellectual curiosity than information technology knowledge. It helps to understand how and why information is published; the channels through which it is communicated; and how, when and by whom it is organized.

# Do your clients often say, "Well, I've already searched the Net. What else could

# you possibly find for me?" or "Why do you charge me so much for this work? Isn't it all on the Net for free?"

Our clients don't ask such blatant questions, but I know many of our clients do use the Net and still come to us for other material. I think we may have lost some clients to the Net, and others to the user-friendly services designed for end users.

If the Net or the other user-friendly packaged services can satisfy all the information needs of our clients, and my clients have the time available to spend searching, then I think I would simply have to accept that. But the reality is that the Net is like one large, important but unpruned and tangled branch of a huge knowledge tree that extends well beyond that single branch. It is not possible to answer all information needs from any single branch of that knowledge tree, even when the technology for doing so is brilliant. Astute information seekers also know how treacherous the Net can be, especially if the provenance of the information is not clear. I remember being absolutely stunned in my first Net training course to be able to find the famous secret Coca-Cola formula. Wow! I thought, the Internet really is fantastic—until I read towards the bottom of the apparently legitimate recipe "Drink at your own risk."

Business and government clients understand that information that has been sold for decades because it had value to its purchasers is not now going to be given away. Most executives now realize that the only information available for free on the Internet, or in their own mailbox at home, is information people are keen to give away. The so-called "gift" may be advertising or company reports, or it may be given away by organizations with a charter to communicate as widely as possible—government departments, consumer groups, political parties and so on. It might be useful information given away because a heavy advertising load subsidizes it. The market research firms and other organizations that spend fortunes collating or checking or indexing data are certainly not going to suddenly become charitable organizations that give that work away for nothing.

The proprietary database services are usually more useful than the Net. Even so, I do not know how any organization could survive by using just one online service. In Australia, one has to have a minimum of two online services, and we use more than ten.

It is maddening, too, when we have to search old magazines manually, when their publishers have whiz-bang Web sites for current information. I wish all publishers of consumer magazines understood the research value of even their old issues. It is in those back issues that we find evidence for court cases, information on how consumer behavior has changed, and so on.

Although in Australia there is enormous interest in the Internet, we are still rather backward in terms of having all major newspapers online for a reasonable archival period. One newspaper, the Hobart *Mercury*, has been taken off-line altogether, and online access to the Melbourne *Herald* has been curtailed to recent years only. Archival issues of *The Bulletin*, a very important magazine for political comment and social issues, have not been available online for a few years.

Coming back to the Internet, it is fascinating how dazzling the technology is and how successfully it has attracted interest from people who are not information professionals. My approach has been to adopt the role of adviser on information sources to clients. I advise clients of useful sites I have come across, but at the same time I raise issues relating to whether information has been refereed, its currency, who authored it, and its reliability. So hopefully our clients will use the Internet wisely and know when they should call us for information that is better obtained from other sources. Using Roger Summit's metaphor, I think it is fine for our clients to wade in the "shallow and sometimes murky water along the shores of the sea of information" as long as they know when it is in their interests to get "into the deeper water where the really big ones are."

# What a great quote, and from the founder of Dialog, no less! When did he say that?

He mentioned it to me when we sat together at an Information Online dinner in Sydney. He came up with the metaphor in a presentation on traditional online services and/or the Internet at the TLS Conference in Stockholm in November 1996.

# Can you walk me through an example of a fun research project you did?

I can't be too revealing about the research we do, but I can describe a search I did some time ago that I found satisfying. A manufacturing company called to ask for information about a relatively new competitor—let's call it ABC. My client was intrigued because ABC had become active in the same market and had announced expansion plans by acquiring a couple of other companies. The rumors in the marketplace, however, suggested that ABC was experiencing financial problems and was suffering substantial losses. My client was interested in learning more about ABC. Was ABC profitable? What were its plans for expansion? If they were experiencing financial difficulties, why were they continuing to expand? Why were they continuing to invest in these activities in Australia?

I knew a little about ABC, as I had seen announcements in the industry journals about them. I knew a large European conglomerate owned them. As a foreign-owned subsidiary, a detailed Annual Return should have been lodged with the Australian Securities and Industry Commission. A quick search in the Commission's Ascot database [6] revealed that the rumors about financial losses were true. They had closed one or two factories and had written off considerable assets. Their acquisitions were clearly strategic, but they were also carrying out a program to cut back expenses.

I searched Australian newspaper databases for reports in the business press and found very little. Clearly the company had not released much information to the Australian press. But from the Annual Return I had noted the company also had a director with a New Zealand address. When I searched the New Zealand business databases, I found the European parent had also acquired companies in New Zealand. So clearly the parent company in Europe had a strategy involving investments in both Australia and New Zealand. I still needed to find out why the company was apparently expanding through acquisition in both Australia and New Zealand when it had incurred such substantial losses, and it appeared as though the losses would continue.

When I searched international databases such as PROMT and Globalbase on Dialog, I found the statements the chairman had made to shareholders at the Annual General Meeting about the company's investments in Australia and New Zealand. The losses were acknowledged, but the long-term strategic plans to use Australia and New Zealand as a point of entry into the huge Asian market were also revealed. Furthermore, an estimate was given of when it was anticipated the new acquisitions would be profitable.

I was able to provide my client with the detailed financial accounts of ABC as well as an outline of the long-term strategic plans for ABC in this region, by using a range of sources. Importantly, some of the information about activities in Australia was easier to find in global sources than in the local press. I also believe it is unlikely that either the parent company or the ABC subsidiary would have announced its strategic plans for Asia on a Web site!

# You build on what you know from one source to find information from another. On another

## topic, when you're done with a search, in what format do you usually deliver it?

Increasingly, we deliver our results as attachments to email messages. If it's small enough, some clients still prefer fax delivery. We deliver spiral-bound reports if the volume of data is too much for fax delivery. For Web pages, we occasionally print pages if appropriate. We also provide the clients with the addresses to Web sites so they can check them out themselves.

## What do you think is in the future for business information professionals?

Some people complete their own income tax returns and make their own investment decisions. Others prefer to rely on experts who usually have additional knowledge and resources. In a similar way, I think there will continue to be a mix of people who want to do their own research by going to libraries, collecting reports or using the Internet. Some, perhaps, will continue to use staff time by sending them to libraries to spend days doing what experts can do in an hour. Others, who recognize that they can be more productive with their own time, will continue to use in-house or external business information professionals to locate important information cost-effectively.

On the whole, I do not feel we will be "overwhelmed" by the Web for serious business research. It is important for business information professionals to be diligent in communicating with clients about the strengths and weaknesses of various information resources.

I think it is exciting that there is so much more interest now in business information as a resource. I feel thrilled when I hear of firms establishing well-planned, well-resourced intranets and introducing "knowledge management." I hope that these firms are the most successful in their own competitive environments.

There are opportunities for those interested in knowledge management. I would like to see more business information professionals being team members in key project areas, contributing their expertise in terms of fast access to critical information.

# Super Searcher Power Tips

▶ Good researchers need to be intelligent, curious, literate, good at algebra, imaginative, persistent, confident, flexible, and they need to like people. It requires more intellectual curiosity than information technology knowledge.

▶ When deciding which among competing online sources to use, I use services that are reliable, fast, current, cost-effective, comprehensive, and where I don't have to remember lots of different passwords and IDs.

▶ The proprietary database services we use are usually more useful than the Net. Even so, I do not know how any organization could survive by using just one online service. One has to have a minimum of two online services, and we use more than ten.

▶ Business information professionals cannot rely on only producing long lists of references or abstracts—it is important to process the information so that key points are extracted and highlighted.

# Bruce Tincknell

## Primary and Secondary Researcher

Bruce Tincknell is the president of Just The Facts, Inc., an independent research company based in Mt. Prospect, IL. Just The Facts offers business intelligence, marketing research and consulting services.

JTFacts@interaccess.com
www.just-the-facts.com

## Tell me about your background and how you started Just The Facts.

My background is different from a lot of people in the industry in that I don't have a formal library background. Everything that I've learned has been through osmosis or trial and error or self-education, although the work experience that fits in nicely is my background in new-product marketing, strategy and research. I worked at a number of large corporations for some twenty-plus years, and at each of those companies I was called upon in some fashion or another to find information. Almost by default I became known as the information guru—"We need to find out about something; get ahold of Bruce." When I worked at Keebler Foods' new ventures group, our charter was to seek out new businesses and develop new products, and especially to find new industries and categories that Keebler could get into, aside from its core business of cookies and crackers. We did a lot of investigation of new industries, new categories, new relationships, new ventures and acquisitions. The president would ask, "What's the frozen food industry like? Tell me all about it. Who are the competitors?

How much do they spend on advertising? What's their market share?" In fact, he wanted a white paper.

Most people hadn't heard of Dialog [20, see Appendix A] in those days, at least outside the library community. I'd read about Dialog somewhere, and I went out and got my own subscription to it. In the beginning, I was doing searching on my own, which was kind of expensive, but then I persuaded the company that this was something beneficial, which they understood pretty quickly.

I have a background in a range of companies—Xerox, divisions of Nestlé, Historic USA (which is a division of a large German confectionery company), and Keebler. I've always been involved in various facets of research and investigating new business areas. That has helped me in my current business, since I've been on the other side, buying research from people, knowing what they're looking for, and why and how it's being used. A lot of times, clients *don't* know how they're going to use the research, or they don't know exactly what they want. It helps to have been in the client's position, sitting across the desk from some executive who says, "This is generally what I want, but I'm not exactly sure what I need. You flesh out the issues." Sometimes it's still trial and error to figure out what the client wants.

It helps to keep in mind that you're trying to find information that makes you say, "Ah! If I were sitting in my client's position, this is what I'd like to know." This puts you in a consultative role. I see a vast distinction between just doing searching and finding information on the one hand, and playing the consultative role and partnering with clients on the other. It's a matter of being solution-oriented as opposed to just seeing yourself as a fact finder.

## When did you start Just The Facts, and what kind of business research are you doing now?

I started the business as something I could do during evenings, weekends and lunch time, while I still had my full-time job. I always wanted to run my own business, and I knew that eventually the corporate world was not going to be the place for me—but we all have to pay the mortgage. So I was doing double duty for a while. After a few years, I left my corporate position and devoted myself full-time to Just The Facts. We're now in our sixth year of continuous business.

In terms of the kind of business research we do, we're a little bit different from the typical secondary search firm out there. We're a combination of a secondary and a primary research company; we're a blend of a business intelligence firm and a traditional marketing research company. By primary research, I mean providing original research—focus groups, trade surveys, interviewing, that sort of thing. And by secondary research, I mean obtaining already-published material—market research reports, company profiles, articles from the trade press, and so on. If you look at research as a continuum, sometimes secondary research is an end in itself, and it answers the client's question. But often, the questions that evolve from secondary research are just the initial part of a project, and clients want secondary information to help guide other parts of a project or research study. In those cases, secondary research is a means to an end.

Having been involved with primary research during my corporate career, I know that there's a lot of information out there. Many times, researchers will use primary research when they could have used secondary; there's so much information available from secondary research that can be useful in guiding primary research. So the issue is to determine what you are trying to accomplish, how you can best and most cost-effectively accomplish your goals, which wheels have already been invented, and which ones you need to invent yourself.

Most companies that do primary research don't have anything to do with secondary, and sometimes they look at secondary sources with a jaundiced eye, which I think is terribly shortsighted. You have different tools to accomplish different jobs. Secondary research is a tool, and if it helps you get to the end result or helps you get there more cost-effectively, why not use it?

# Can you walk through an example of a typical research project?

There is no typical project from our vantage point, but I can give you an example or two.

A company came to us because they were interested in doing business in India. Before they got started, they wanted to know everything they could find out about the country itself. That included the politics, the culture, the economy, business forecasts, corruption issues (which can be important in some foreign countries), business dealings, how people work with one another, how they work with foreigners—or don't, as the case might be. We did a lot of secondary work, initially, and put together a study that identified all the major issues about India that would be helpful to someone who knew very little about the country. This secondary research takes you just so far and then you have to employ a different methodology, and we employed phone work at that point. We talked to people both inside and outside India who were intimately familiar with the culture and confirmed or denied some of the secondary information that we had obtained.

This turned out to be a multiphased project. After reviewing the whole country and the dynamics of doing business in that country, we were asked to identify joint venture partners in a particular category that our client wanted to be in. We identified a variety of joint ventures through telephone interviews. Once we had established a laundry list, we drilled down to the six or eight parties that looked like they might be potential partners. Then we did a rather extensive profiling of potential joint ventures, again through secondary and telephone research.

# How do you know when you've gone as far as you can in a project? How do you set the outer boundaries to a research job?

A lot of that's dictated by the client, and that's why the qualifying interview is so important. Some people from the library end of the business call it the reference interview; we call it "developing the wish list." We'll say to our clients, "Envision what your ideal final outcome would be from us, and tell us what would be in there." In other words, what are the client's expectations? It's important to get them to talk through the project, because a lot of times, they haven't thought it through. Or you find you have an associate—an intermediary—who's calling on behalf of a boss, and they don't exactly know what's going through the ultimate requester's mind. The process is like that party game, one person starts a message and it goes around the circle and by the time it comes to the end of the circle, the message is completely different from when it started. The challenge is really understanding what it is the requester or the ultimate client wants. You could be one-hundred-percent off, if you're not careful, and could give the client something that they don't want, too much or too little, totally in the wrong direction or with the wrong nuance. Having a good ear and asking the right questions up front are critical.

There are times where you go through that process and you *still* make mistakes. The intermediary comes to you with a request, and you're expected to be a mind reader. If you knew the person intimately, you might have some sense of what they're really looking for, but when you're trying to read the mind of somebody you've never met, it approaches clairvoyance—and few of us have the gift.

The other issue is knowing when to stop. If you haven't found out from the client what it is they want and what they expect to get from you, it's like working on two different planes in space. Their expectations are at one level, and your understanding of their needs is at another level, and you're going to fly right past each other.

Understanding that is so important, and that in turn dictates what depth and breadth you go to in the research.

## Do you have a gut sense that you've gotten about as much as you're going to from a particular source? How do you know that you've found the good stuff and it's time to move on?

It comes back to understanding as best you can what your client is looking for. A lot of it certainly is trial and error, but it's also experience-based. Projects tend to fall into groups, so over time you get a sense of whether these answers are fulfilling what the client is seeking. There are always nuances, of course, but in general there is a kind of historical sensory perception that evolves over time, after you've been doing it for a while. There are still times, though, when you're fooled. You think, "Boy, this is *it*," and the client looks at it and says "No, that's really not what we're looking for." We always spell out with clients up front that it may not be possible to get everything they're looking for. We talk about it in terms of probabilities; we say there's a lower probability of getting this information but there's a higher chance of getting something else.

## That's the advantage of describing your initial interview as a wish list. Then it's understood that this is not an order form that you will simply take to the stockroom and fill, but that you'll see what information is out there.

We always try to get the wish list in writing, either faxed or emailed to us. Some people are a little put out and will say, "You're asking me to duplicate what I just told you. I don't have time to do that, I'm *telling* you what I want." Well, there are two reasons for our asking to get the request in writing. Number one, they're usually talking fast or they're in a hurry, and they tend to describe their research needs in a stream of consciousness. You take notes as quickly as you can while they're talking, but you want to make sure you didn't miss anything. Number two, when you force them to put things down in writing, sometimes it helps focus their thoughts as to what they really do want. The real questions can then change or evolve dramatically.

There's a whole other aspect in terms of liability. We want to make sure that, if somebody comes back and says, "That's not what I asked for," we have something in writing that spells out what they did ask for. Fortunately, very few clients do that, but you try to eliminate it altogether through this process. Again, we find that when it does happen—when there's the greatest disconnect—it's usually an intermediary who's been placed in an uncomfortable position. They are going to look bad to their boss or to their internal client, so they don't ask the questions up front that would help clarify the project. You've sent them the work, you've met the timetable and the objectives that they've stated, and when they give it to their superior or client, their boss looks at it and says, "This isn't what I wanted." When that happens, you have to decide how good a client they are, whether this is a client you want to keep, and so on. Sometimes you can spend a lot of time trying to achieve a satisfaction level that just isn't achievable. Clients come with different expectation levels. Some are thrilled with one level, whereas for another client it's totally unacceptable. Managing clients' expectations is absolutely critical.

# How has the expansion of information on the Internet changed how you do secondary research? Are you finding that you're going to the Internet for things that you used to go to Dialog for, or are you just using the

# Internet for new sources of information that aren't available elsewhere?

Obviously, the Internet is evolving, in some cases not quickly enough. From a search engine standpoint, they are not very sophisticated vis-à-vis Dialog or Nexis [40] or Dow Jones [21]. And there's always the issue of time versus cost versus value.

I hear clients say, "I've already done secondary searching. I've been on the Internet." The perception is that the Internet has it all and you can basically find it all yourself, so why call a researcher to do research? The Internet is as much a help as a hindrance sometimes. The best clients are those who have spent time doing some Net searching and haven't found a thing. They come to you and say, "I know I've done all the searching that can possibly be done, but is there some scrap somewhere you might find?" At that point, they begin to understand the value of our services.

We see an evolving trend in senior management; they are looking at the Internet as both a blessing and a curse. On the one hand, there are some good things about it, but people are wasting an awful lot of time when they ought to be doing the key aspects of their job. Rather than looking at the Internet as "everything you need, for free," they're finding out that it's taking an enormous amount of time to find information. The bottom line is: What's the value of your time? Is it worth so little that you can afford to spend five, ten, twenty hours searching around? Meanwhile, if you're a marketing person or HR person or whatever, what are you doing with the other parts of your job? The Internet is still new, and everybody wants to be able to say that they know how to "surf the Web."

We use the Internet, but we use it judiciously. We look at a project and decide where the likely benefits are or where the likely sources of this type of information are; it's all a judgment call in the end.

# When you do search the Internet, do you usually use one of the search engines or do you have a list of bookmarks or sites that you normally go to first?

It's dictated by the type of project. We do a fair amount of company profiling, where somebody wants to know about a particular business, and there are some sites that are useful for that. Other times, it's just going to call for some trolling. The size of the project determines how much time you can spend doing that kind of thing, but in general we don't look at the Internet as the first choice. I see it as a good supplement; we've got our bag of tools, and the Internet is one more tool we can use. Sometimes it's broad searching, and sometimes it's very focused.

# By the same token, do you have any files that you always use on Dialog or the other professional online services?

Again, that's project driven because different projects necessitate different approaches—even the decision of one system versus another, Dialog versus Nexis versus Dow Jones. Everything comes back to the decision maker, the expectations and the wish list—that's the focal point, that's what's driving the project. It's only through time and experience that you learn which sources are going to be most helpful for a given type of project. Even then it can change, depending upon the nuances of the project.

We're like a doctor in that you go to a doctor with a problem. With us, you're coming to the information doctor with a problem or a need. We make a diagnosis in each individual situation, and while one person might have the same condition as another person, there may be differences that require different prescriptions. One person has high blood pressure, the other doesn't. By the same token, each project is different. Just because you've used Dialog's files 9, 15,

16, and 148 *[Editor's note: Business & Industry, ABI/Inform, IAC PROMT, and IAC Business & Industry Database]* on one project, say, that doesn't mean they're going to be appropriate for the next one. You have to make a determination and use your judgment in each situation; it shouldn't be an autopilot approach.

## Doctors read the *Journal of the American Medical Association* to stay on top of medical news. How do you stay on top of news on the information industry related to business research?

I try to carve out a certain amount of time per week for what I refer to as refreshment, if you will; that's learning time for me. It might be just poking around in a certain database or in a new service. I read a very diverse set of journals and information sources, trying to soak up as much as I can. You can always do more, but time is the issue when you're trying to run a business.

## Do you subscribe to any electronic discussion groups?

I subscribe to AIIP-L [61]. Even with just that one, I have so much to wade through, and the issue becomes time. You could take a good chunk of your day just following up and sorting through your email.

## Have you noticed that more of your clients are expecting results electronically, or are you still doing a lot of hard-copy delivery?

It depends. Some clients want the information yesterday and they want it emailed. But I would say that eighty percent or more still want hard copy. The reason is that providing information is one thing, but providing it in presentation form is another—and you have to think of the information as a package. At least part of the value of information is in the presentation. If you went to the grocery store and all of the items in the store were out of their packages on the shelf, you wouldn't put the same value on those products as you would if they were nicely presented. And so it is with our research.

Companies that just offer data dumps, rip and ship, often aren't profitable businesses. If someone is just doing that, they're going to have to do an awful lot of volume to be profitable. I'm not saying that it's right or wrong, but you have to determine what kind of business you want to be in and what you want to provide to your customer. And part of the delivery issue is the question of packaging. While there *are* clients who just want email, we try to discourage that. You may be dealing with an intermediary, and your project will be going to the ten key executives in the company. If you deliver it electronically and the intermediary prints it out, the formatting and presentation can get lost and it might wind up reflecting poorly on you. In those cases, the intermediary is going to feel sheepish about delivering an unprofessional-looking project and will say, "Okay, we'll never use *them* again," instead of admitting that they just didn't know how to print out the report properly. Let's face it, the corporate world being what it is, people don't want to fall on their own sword: they want to survive, and that means protecting their backsides.

The way we look at it, we want to present our work in the best light, but we want our intermediary to appear in the best light too. So we try, as much as possible, to present the final product in a finished hard-copy form.

## What do you see as the future of the information professional? Where do you think we'll be in five years?

I'm very optimistic, as long as we're adding intellectual value to our products. If you're not adding value, then you're nowhere in the long term. There's lots of pure price competition if you're just out there finding facts. What sets researchers apart is their interpretation of the information and the value they add to it. And that comes from their experience, from their knowledge base, from their ability to interpret what their client wants. If you're looking at your job as just providing facts and figures, then you are in a vulnerable position in the long run. There's always going to be a segment that looks at what you do and says, "I could do that on the Internet." If they don't see you as more than just a fact finder, then I think you're at tremendous risk.

**It sounds to me like what you're saying is that we need to differentiate ourselves from what's available on the Net generally, and to show how far removed we are from that kind of data dump.**

Right. If people believe that all you're really doing is just basic searching, then they don't see the value because they think it's something anyone can do. Most people will make the leap and say, "I'm just as smart or smarter than you are, and I have my M.B.A. or M.A. or Ph.D. or whatever, so why do I need you?" That's why positioning and marketing yourself in terms of who you are, why you're different and what you bring to the party is so critical. Without that, you're just another fact finder. On the other hand, people recognize that there's value in consultative points of view—what does this data mean, what are the ramifications of this information. Our clients are coming to us not because we can gather information but because of our expertise in pulling it all together and interpreting what it means, why this is important, and how it will impact their decision making.

The other aspect of what we offer is the convenience factor. It's the difference between a convenience store and a grocery store. Most people recognize that convenience stores charge higher prices, but they're willing to shop there because they know they're quick and they're convenient; *that* provides value. They know that they're going to pay an extra quarter or fifty cents for a carton of milk or a loaf of bread, but customers recognize that their time is worth something and they don't want to stand in a long line at the grocery store. It's the same for information professionals. The value we're providing is the convenience factor. Our clients don't have to spend their time doing the searching themselves. As a result, they can focus on the truly significant responsibilities of their job.

## That's a tough sell sometimes, isn't it?

Yes. We get a lot of people who call up and want to know how much something is going to cost. Almost one hundred percent of the time, we require what we call exploratory searching before we can answer a question. We'll say, "We don't know how much is out there and we can't really guess but we'll spend, say, one or two hours at a cost of XYZ to come back and tell you what's available. Are you going to get actual information from this initial search? No, you're not. What you're going to get is a diagnosis from us about what we think may be available, how much it's going to cost to get it, and how long it's going to take to find it." When you go to the doctor, the meter's running the minute you set foot in the doctor's office, regardless of what he finds. Likewise, we're going to do exploratory searching and come back with a diagnosis and a prescription. We have to put on a consultative hat, as opposed to just a fact-finding hat.

Related to that, we're always looking for good people to hire, and it's hard to find people who have information-gathering skills *and* a business background. Without that business background, how can you talk with your clients and understand why they need this information? I think it's a great disservice that the library schools are doing to their students in this day and age, that they aren't working with the business schools of their universities, and they aren't incorporating business or competitive intelligence aspects into their programs. We see people who are very good from a library background, but they don't have the business background to go along with it. It's a shame that the library schools aren't building partnerships with business schools. There is the possibility of some great cross-pollination, but it's not just the library school departments. The business schools don't recognize the need for information-gathering and secondary research skills, either.

# Super Searcher Power Tips

► I see a vast distinction between just searching and retrieving information on the one hand and playing the consultative role and partnering with clients on the other.

► There's lots of competition if you're just finding the facts. What sets researchers apart is their interpretation of the information and the value that they add to it.

► It's only through time and experience that you learn which sources are going to be most helpful for a given type of project, and even then it can change, depending upon the nuances of the project.

# Anne Caputo
## Vendor Liaison and Instructor

Anne Caputo is the Assistant Director
for InfoPro and Academic Programs
for Dow Jones Interactive Publishing.
She is based in Washington, DC.

anne.caputo@dowjones.com

**I've known you for years in your former capacity as a Dialog liaison for information professionals. Can you give a little history about how you started out in this field and where you are now?**

The most important thing to tell others about me is that I am a librarian, in the sense that I have an M.L.S., which I obtained from San Jose State University back in the '70-somethings. I went to library school because I wanted to be an archivist and a museum librarian, and I wanted to have absolutely nothing to do with computers whatsoever. When I got out of library school, I discovered there wasn't a hot market for people who wanted to do what I thought I wanted to do, and I went to my advisor, Martha West, who said to me, "There's this little research project called Dialog that deals with information retrieval down there at Lockheed. You ought to go down there and be interviewed." So I got in my Volkswagen Beetle with the Save-the-Whales bumper stickers, and I drove down there. It just so happened that I arrived on the day that the Stanford University students were picketing Lockheed with "Merchant of Death" signs. I wanted to say to them, "Hey, I'm one of you. I'm not Miss Buttoned-Down-Zipped-Up-Military-Research-Type Person. But on the other hand, I need a job. I'm just going to fly right through here and park."

I went in and was interviewed, and I knew nothing about what they were talking about. I mean *nothing*. They had built Dialog [20, see Appendix A] and were just beginning to try to market it. I didn't know what Dialog was. I had never seen a Silent 700 terminal before. The interviewer kept saying, "And you would earn 10K," and I kept thinking, "What's a 'K'?" This was not a good sign.

Evidently, during the course of the interview, I said several things that were right. One of them was that I had been a high school teacher, so I had teaching and instructional experience on a very tough audience level. I also had been the Oregon high-school debate champion my senior year of high school, which said I had experience thinking on my feet. I believe that those two attributes got me hired. Those things got me the job, and for the rest of it, he said, "Well, you can learn that. And by the way, in two weeks you'll be teaching others." I was maybe the seventh employee overall—and the first woman—to work directly on the program.

So I arrived at work, and they said: "This is the telephone, and it's hooked up to an 800 number that has just been publicized this week, and when it rings you're customer service. And when it's not ringing, you're the newsletter editor. And when you're not doing that, you're writing the training material. And when you're not doing any of those things, you can go out and do training." So the phone rang, and it was somebody calling for the venereal disease hotline because Dialog's 800 number had been used for that purpose prior to Dialog.

Over many excruciating weeks, during which every single thing people asked me I had to find out about, someone finally called up and asked me a question I had answered before, and I thought, "Maybe I can do this."

So I came into this having no background or preparation. Remember, it was a time when hardly anybody had that experience and we were willing to work for 10K—which I found out was my salary, and there were three zeros after the ten. So that's how it started. I had never actually been a working librarian other than as an intern in library school.

But time passed, and they hired other people of my kind, and I came to Washington, DC. I was told that I was going to be the business information specialist, which was interesting because what did I know about business information? So that was my next job—learning enough about the content of business databases and what people doing business searching *did*, in order to teach them things that would be helpful. That was one of my variety of jobs at Dialog. I also worked on the library school program and the classroom instruction program and, more recently, the Quantum professional development and outreach program for librarians and information professionals.

Parallel to this, starting in 1977, I also took on the job of being an instructor at Catholic University in the School of Library and Information Science. I'm on the adjunct faculty, and I've been there for twenty-one years.

In September of 1998, I left Dialog after twenty-two-plus years, and went to work for Dow Jones Interactive Publishing [21] doing similar things. I was recruited by Tim Andrews because Dow Jones is interested in having a higher presence in the information professional community and they wanted somebody who could help them go to the next level. So that's where I am now.

# This job probably wasn't quite as hard to figure out as your first job, was it?

No. It has its moments, but they're better moments. There are two things at Dow Jones that are important to do, and they're important to do at the same time. Qne is to help create a library school or classroom instruction program aimed primarily at information professionals, and also at students in business schools—and in a more tangential way, maybe journalism students. Tim Andrews told me that the thing he hated most about Dialog was that every time Dow Jones people walked into a library customer's office, the customer said, "I learned Dialog in library school and it's still my favorite system. You'll have to wean me away from that." So for me at Dow Jones, a major priority is to create some presence in the information professional community. I think we recognize we're not going to bump Dialog or Nexis [40] in the first go-around, but we want to be a player on that level as soon as possible.

Related to that, when the students graduate and become information professionals, the goal is to make them understand that a vendor can also be their partner. The vendor is not only somebody who sells them something, but is there after the sale is complete. And they are partners not only in installation and training and support, but also in other professional arenas. Partners who can help with questions like: How do you measure return on investment? How do you interface with your information technology people? How do you create a marketing plan and present it to senior management? Things that we know or can learn from our customers or from other professional affiliations. It's incumbent on us to do that if we really want to be what we say we are—that is, their full partner.

## So you're sort of giving advice on how to run a small business, or run a business within a business.

That's right. And how to maintain that level of presence, and how to really say to customers that what you know is so valuable and so important and so much in the mainstream of what's happening in the world of business today. Don't hide that under a stack of catalog cards. Go out there and shine. You may have to use different words to describe what you do, because people don't know that "collection development" really is looking on the Internet and determining what's appropriate, what's right and what fits into our needs. All these things that we thought were passé now become more important than ever. We have those skills, by gum, and we'd better make sure that our management knows that.

**There are so many new ways of answering questions that we couldn't do four or five years ago. It used to be like the saying that if all you have is a hammer, everything looks like a nail. All of a sudden we've got all kinds of tools, and now we're trying to figure out all the ways to use them. What impact do you think the Net has had on how business researchers find information and even on how they frame the question?**

I think your metaphor of tools and hammer is very apt, because I always tell my students that everything they're learning goes into their tool kit. There are big tools; and there are small, fine-detail tools; and there are tools you use a lot that are lying on the top; and there are tools that you just need to know are there when you have a special job. Their role is to understand those tools and know when to use the appropriate one. About two or two-and-a-half years ago, for the very first time, I walked into class and had to go through a routine that said, "This is why you have to learn all of this stuff in this class. This is not an Internet plug-it-in, pull-it-out class. This is a full-blown information-retrieval class with lots of different tools, *including* the Internet."

In the past, I never used to say, "This is why you have to learn to use Dialog or Nexis or whatever system you happen to be using." Lately, I actually have to draw on the blackboard a schematic of the content sea, the ocean of content, and draw a dinghy and a medium-size tanker and a giant cargo ship, and say: "Here are all the boats floating on the content sea. The content, in many cases, is the same. It's the same water that they're all in, but each of these vessels has different tools to mine and find what you want. If you want the ocean of what's on the top, any one will work. But if you want to be an ocean miner and go down to the bottom and sift through the whole series of levels, then you really have to have a powerful system, and a dinghy ain't gonna make it. In the world we see right now—maybe not forever but certainly right now—the Internet is the dinghy. It's floating on a lot of content, but its mining tools are not very sophisticated, so it should be integrated in with all the other tools you have."

And they're sitting there in their rows of desks with their mouths hanging open saying, "Oh, I thought this was going to be an easy course. I can do the Internet, why do I need to know *that*?" And by the end, most of them think, "Wow, now I am *really* prepared to be a competitor out there." In fact, this fall, someone who was in my class a year ago came in and said, "I just want to get down on my knees and kiss the hem of your skirt because I was scared to death and I thought I could never do this, and now I have this great job and what you said is really true." That hasn't happened much in twenty years, but it probably happens without being expressed more than you might think. The pain of learning the systems really is worth it. The Internet is a great tool. I increasingly use it and I've taught it in the class for the last couple of years, but it is not the only tool.

**It's startling to think about having to promote to library school students that they should be taking an online class. When I was in library school, it was offered, but almost in the context of "Oh, you guys may not need to take all this new-fangled Dialog stuff."**

# When you teach your students about online services, do you see any of them as a natural first place for business researchers to start?

From a teaching point of view, I start with Dialog. I have traditionally done that, and I plan to continue to do so, because I think it's important to see a system that reveals the way it works. The hood is up and we're looking at the engine working more closely in classic Dialog than in any other service. It's very important to see what sets look like, what happens when you use different kinds of connectors, how you can increase or decrease retrieval, what an "expand" list looks like and how revealing that can be about the quality and content of databases—or lack thereof, in some cases—and so on. So we start with Dialog. I've toyed with the idea of starting with the Internet, and I've toyed with starting with an end-user-oriented system, but I still go back to teaching them Dialog first.

Then I usually have both a Nexis speaker and a Dow Jones speaker come in and give a lecture on those services. And then I give them a two-unit series on the Internet, starting with simple things and moving to more complex capabilities. They learn a variety of Internet pathways, such as AltaVista [2] and Northern Light [47]. I use a service called Highway 61 [29], which I find interesting; it's a librarian-built system, which I like as well. Most of them know HotBot [31], Yahoo! [60], Excite [25] and all the standard places, so I try not to dwell on things they already know.

# I've noticed that a lot of people are going less and less to search engines and more and more to either catalogs like Yahoo! or subject guides. It seems that we're re-intermediating, as it were, asking for someone to pull the good stuff together into libraries and files

## and databases just like the professional online services we librarians are used to.

Exactly. We're getting ready to do the Internet unit now, and I would predict that most people who were great Internet searchers when they started the course will now say, "Is this all it can do? Is this what I have to go through to get where I want to go?" I think those sites that have formed collections—that would include things like the Dow Jones Web Center—that are pre-selected, "certified" Web sites are doing a service that people will increasingly find useful.

## How do you tell people to think through a search? Say they get a question on the market for aluminum widgets. How do you suggest that they approach it? How do they start their search, how do they know that they're on the right track, and how do they know when they've found enough?

Those are profound questions for students, especially for those who think "there is a right answer and I have to find it." That's a process that's painful for them. They don't like open-ended questions. They like the ready-reference factual questions because they know that it's either black or white. This business of doing open-ended research is very, very difficult for them. We have to spend a lot of time talking about precision and recall—in other words, an understanding that eternity is not long enough to find everything, that you've got to know when enough is enough.

I make them do a reference interview several different times, starting with a reference interview of themselves, setting up an information need that they have, whether it's the number of businesses in Durham, North Carolina, that they could work for, or more esoteric types of things. They have to set up a checklist and ask themselves questions from the checklist. And the questions are: How many do I expect to find? What kind of answer is ideal? What would be acceptable if what I'm looking for is not found?—the whole standard routine. Is it in English? Is it this type of document or that? How would I know a right answer if I saw it? Once they've done that exercise for *themselves*, so they understand why the questions are being asked, then they have to do a full-blown reference interview with somebody else for their final search project. It makes them understand that what people ask for is not necessarily what they really want, that they can't always articulate off the bat what they really want, that the element of serendipity is very powerful, and that they will show their patron things and the patron will say, "Oh, yeah, that's what I meant!" "Well, why didn't you say that?" "Because I didn't know how to say that."

So I am very strong on reference interview skills, and I make them do that a lot, and I'm sure they don't like that too much. But it's powerful, and it also shows them that there are many right answers. What is not so real to them, but what they'll learn later, is the impact of cost on all of this, because this is like Monopoly money to them; they don't have to pay for it yet. Even though the services they use give them cost indications, typically it's not real money, and they don't understand that as well now as they will eventually. I can give them a time budget, but they still sort of think it doesn't really matter. "She said $500 and I spent $5,000, but who cares?"

I tell them to start by learning everything they think might help them. So there's a little blank section on their search form that says: Do a brain dump. Here's what you already know. Do you know people who write in this field? Do you know associations in this field? Do you know publications or conferences or whatever in this field? Do you know if there's a ton of information available, or hardly any?

Then I typically tell them to start with a global search on a value-added vendor, like Dialog's Dialindex, just to get a sense of where things will come up. That's often surprising to them. "Oh, gosh, I didn't know there'd be something in a geology database," or "I didn't know there'd be something in a mental health database." They're not looking at the content so much as getting a feeling for its scattering and spread. It also helps them understand unusual meanings of the terms, acronyms that have different meanings, all the stuff that can be fatal if you don't realize it early on. And then when they know more, I tell them to go out and do an Internet browse of some sort, looking for the same kind of thing. That gives them enough information to go back for the second conversation with their client. I make them have two in-detail talks: the going-in talk and the "now that I know more, here's what I would ask now" talk.

## Are there any other searching tips you give your students?

I would say know your sources, and know the ones that have really pulled through for you and have been reliable for you in the past. Be willing to look at new sources, but always know the really good sources that have been there for you. I'm thinking of PROMT and ABI/Inform, for example—the ones that we know have quality content and are well indexed. Rely on those and be open to new things.

From a vendor perspective, I think it's easy to get into the trap of making the interface appropriate for non-power searchers. Dow Jones has taken the interface issue to heart, and I think we're on the right track. We just need to stay focused on that track. That would be true for other vendors as well. Northern Light is clearly beginning to see that you have to build power tools and not mask them with a lot of drop-down menus. Give the power searchers the opportunity to use that great knowledge and skill that they have, and you'll be rewarded with a system that will have great return on investment in the power searcher audience.

## I'm thinking back to your analogy of floating on this sea of information. Since it's often the

# same information in several different places or formats, how do you decide which one of those to use?

Well, my disclaimer is that I live in an artificial world in that regard, because I've never, ever in my life had to actually pay for anything I use online. While I think about price, which is probably uppermost for many people, it's not uppermost in my mind, although I'm clearly mindful of it. I would say that you go to the medium where you get the biggest bang. For example, I would not buy something on CD-ROM if I could get it online, unless there was a very compelling reason to do that, an accessibility reason or a pricing reason or something like that. I would say go where you have the greatest connectivity, or the greatest amount of clustered information that you need to use, whether it's vendor X or vendor Y. I find switching back and forth—the mental process of figuring out how the interface works—very difficult. And speaking as some-body who works for an aggregator, the bigger aggregator wins. Dow Jones is not the biggest aggregator, but we are working on being it in our selected fields of endeavor, for example. And Dialog, of course, is the king of the aggregators, traditionally. So I say go where you get the biggest bang.

# How do you stay updated on new systems and services? How do you watch your competitive environment?

Just keeping up on what Dow Jones is doing is as challenging to me as it is to anybody walking in the door. I have a very broad elec-tronic clipping file on all of the major competitors. I'd rather get more than less, because I really like to see what's going on. So I have several clips of things that I'm interested in tracking.

Then I try to pay attention to several trade journals, particularly certain columns or certain writers. So I have a clipping file on

Barbara Quint, you, Reva Basch, Marydee Ojala and Sue Feldman, and a few other people whose opinions I think are important. I subscribe to *Online* [92], *Searcher* [94], *Database* [77] and *Information Today* [88], and I just carry them around in my briefcase so when I'm on a plane I can look at them. At least once a week, I look at the Information Today [34] and Online Inc. [48] Web sites for breaking news. I find that the Information Today Web site has breaking news faster, and Barbara Quint often has an insightful paragraph or two on it as well.

And here's my secret weapon: When I go to professional conferences, I hang around in the ladies' room and listen to what other people are talking about. I don't hang out there a lot, but when I'm in there I'm listening to what other people are talking about. People used to think the men's room was the place where business got transacted, and women were huddled around the outside hoping that some of it would spill over. Well, now I think the ladies' room is where things happen. If you need something, you can go in there and say, "I wonder how I could get a ..." and ten people will run up and tell you how to do it. It is an extremely valuable resource.

## Times have changed, haven't they? We're doing the same thing in person that we do on the librarians' electronic discussion groups. Speaking of which, do you subscribe to any electronic mailing lists?

I used to be on Buslib [63] but eventually it got to be too much. Some of it's interesting, but I haven't got time to read it every day. Barb Burton, another Dow Jones InfoPro person, has scanning software that monitors thirty-five different lists—some very active and some that are fairly quiet. She looks for mentions of several things—Dow Jones certainly is one of them, but some other topics as well—and she only sees those messages that she has prescreened as being interesting. She reads those and any that she thinks are more globally interesting she passes along. So I would say I get two or three messages a day. It's a trade-off, of course. We may miss some things with the screening, but at least we know when Dow Jones is being mentioned because we have to respond, or at least know about it.

# How do you deal with the situation when a patron says "I've done a Lexis-Nexis search, so don't bother going there," or "I've already done an Internet search—what else can you find me?"

I tell my students that if they have a client who says, "I've done XYZ already, don't bother," they should either do it and not tell the client they did it, or if they need to say something to the client, they should say, "I'm sure you have and I'm sure you found very valuable information, but I need to educate myself. I need to be aware of the process that you've gone through, too, so it can help me do a better search for you using other resources." Whether it's openly or not, I tell them they need to do it. I hope they will realize that their client probably didn't know how to do a search well, or did miss things. You can say, "You know, I've got a lot of little tricks up my sleeve that I've learned over the past thousand searches that I've done. I might just try a couple of things that you might not have thought of."

# I sometimes tell my clients that any two people searching the same resource will inevitably find a different set of materials,

# so this is just my way of increasing the odds that we'll get all the good stuff.

My students can see that clearly because there are typically twelve of them in a room all doing the same assignment. We get to the discussion part and I hear, "Well, I did it this way." "Well, I did it that way." "Well, I found this." "Well, I found that." In the end I say, "And which is better?" and they realize. Very few people learn this except in the library school setting, where they get the experience of having ten or twelve people all doing the same search and then comparing results, because that's not part of nature. They often say, "Well, how would the experts do it?" Or "How would a really good searcher do it?" And I say, "You get twenty of them in here, I'll bet you you'd get twenty versions of this."

# How do you deal with the areas that the Net isn't real strong on yet, like knowing ownership of the material, knowing that the material will be around in a year? What do you suggest to them when they find good information on a business site, but aren't assured that the information will remain available for long?

I make them document where they found it and when, so that at least they know it was there at that particular time. I tell them that, if it has to be authoritative, you have to go to authoritative sources. I still think of the Net as adding to the material they get from a value-added service—things that a value-added service will never have, like information from a company's home page on their competitive stance. So they need to think of the Net as the additional information that fills out the entire picture, but is not the heart of the picture. It's too risky to base the heart of what you do on something that may be ephemeral.

## That's especially hard to keep in mind when their exposure to the Internet before that class was probably, "Gosh, I can find so much cool information" without the thought of "But what if I need to produce it again in two months?"

Or what if you went into court and somebody said, "How do you know that?" and you said, "Well, I got it off company X's Web page." What do you think the judge and jury are going to say? Would you risk big-time stakes on it? I don't think so. At least the company's own Web site is authoritative insofar as that's what they want the world to know. On the other hand, sometimes they have techies doing the Web site content and they may be telling the world more than the world ought to know. "Oh, I've got this org chart, let's put that up on the Web site!"

## What kind of personality do you think makes a good online searcher?

I always tell my students that people who like to solve puzzles make good online searchers—anything that involves a stepwise process toward an end, that isn't just jumping from here to there. People who like the process of doing crossword puzzles, jigsaw puzzles, word puzzles, playing puzzle-type games are people who are going to be good online searchers, because they find that the process is as interesting as the end. For them, getting the process right is a reward in itself. The ultimate reward, of course, is doing a good job and making money for your company or earning your client's fee, or whatever it might be.

# What do you find most frustrating about online research?

Things that frustrate me change over time. Historically, one of the most frustrating things was the difficulty in choosing the best source for the answer. Cross-file indexes and the diminished emphasis on having to choose databases and sources have lessened that frustration. My current irritant is the slowness of the Internet and the proliferation of "unbranded" sources that may or may not be authoritative.

# Where do you think the future of the business information professional is going? Are we going to be totally outdated by everyone searching the Internet for free?

Since I'm in the business of selling to information profession-als and teaching information professionals, I don't think that's the case. But I will say that those who are not smart and adaptable will find themselves as obsolete as dodo birds. It's not a given that, because we know all these great things and have these great skills, we're going to still be in a position to have good jobs. It's our role to define what we can do with our knowledge and to sell that, because I don't think it's apparent in the business paradigm today. A lot of leaders don't realize that what we know is incred-ibly valuable, and it's up to us to make that case.

It comes down to that old saying, think outside the box. Use dif-ferent terminology. Describe your skills in terms and ways that your audience can understand—even though they're not library terms—and show them where we go to the bottom line, where being "infor-mation smart" is going to make money or save money. It's interest-ing to be able to do all these online searches, but unless we're focused on the business case, it isn't going to matter. We're either going to be out of a job or inside an organization, making a case for how we add value to the information. And we'd all rather be inside making "Ks."

# Super Searcher Power Tips

▶ It's important to say to customers that what you know is valuable and so much in the mainstream of what's happening in the world of business today. Don't hide that under a stack of catalog cards—go out there and shine.

▶ I am very strong on reference interview skills; they're powerful skills and they remind you that there are many right answers.

▶ I usually recommend starting with a Dialog Dialindex search, not to look at the content so much as to get a feeling for its scattering and spread. It helps you understand unusual meanings of terms and acronyms that have different meanings—things that could be fatal to your search if you don't realize them early on.

▶ When selecting which information resource to use, go where you have the greatest connectivity, or the greatest amount of clustered information. I find switching back and forth—the mental process of figuring out how the interface works—to be very difficult.

▶ People who like to solve puzzles make good online searchers—anything that involves a stepwise process toward an end that isn't just jumping from here to there.

# Appendix A:
## Referenced Sites and Sources

### Internet Sites and Online Databases

1. **ABC News**
abcnews.go.com

2. **AltaVista**
www.altavista.com

3. **Amazon.com**
www.amazon.com

4. **American Society of Association Executives (ASAE)**
www.asaenet.org

5. **Anzwers**
www.anzwers.com.au

6. **Ascot**
www.search.asc.gov.au

7. **Ausinet**
ausinet.fairfax.com.au

8. **Australian Bibliographic Network**
www.nla.gov.au/abn/

9. **Books in Print**
www.booksinprint.com

10. **Bowling Green University Library of Popular Culture**
www.bgsu.edu/colleges/library/pcl/pcl.html

11. **CareerMosaic**
www.careermosaic.com

12. **CBS News**
www.cbsnews.com

13. **CDB Infotek**
www.cdb.com

14. **Census Bureau**
www.census.gov

15. **Cinch**
(produced by Informit Online)
www.informit.com.au

16. **CIT**
www.citgroup.com

17. **CNBC/Dow Jones Business Video**
www.msnbc.com/m/v/video_news.asp

18. **CorpTech**
www.corptech.com

19. **Deja News**
www.deja.com

20. **Dialog**
www.dialog.com

21. **Dow Jones Interactive**
djinteractive.com

22. **Dun & Bradstreet**
www.dnb.com

23. **EDGAR**
edgar.sec.gov

24. **Encyclopedia of Associations**
www.gale.com

25. **Excite**
www.excite.com

26. **Family**
(produced by Informit Online)
www.informit.com.au

27. **Frost & Sullivan**
www.frost.com

28. **Global Access**
www.disclosure.com

29. **Highway 61**
www.highway61.com

30. **Hoover's**
www.hoovers.com

31. **HotBot**
hotbot.lycos.com

32. **IAC InSite**
www.iac-insite.com

33. **Information America**
www.infoam.com

34. **Information Today**
    www.infotoday.com

35. **Informit Online**
    www.informit.com.au

36. **InterNIC**
    www.internic.net

37. **Investext**
    www.investext.com

38. **Kinetica**
    www.nla.gov.au/kinetica

39. **Kompass**
    www.kompass.com

40. **Lexis-Nexis**
    www.lexis-nexis.com

41. **Manning & Napier**
    www.mnis.net

42. **Monster Board**
    www.monsterboard.com

43. **National Association of Securities Dealers**
    www.nasdr.com

44. **NBC News**
    www.nbc.com

45. **Net Partners**
    www.netpartners.com

46. **NewsPage**
    www.individual.com

47. **Northern Light**
    www.northernlight.com

48. **Online Inc.**
    www.onlineinc.com

49. **Outsourcing Institute**
    www.outsourcing.com

50. **PACER** (Public Access to Court Electronic Records program)
    pacer.psc.uscourts.gov
    For more information, call the PACER service center at 800/676-6856.

51. **Presscom**
    www.presscom.com.au

52. **Questel/Orbit**
    www.questel.orbit.com

53. **Reuters Business Briefing**
    www.reuters.com/rbb

54. **SEC Edgar** list of files
edgar.sec.gov/edaux/forms.htm

55. **Standard & Poor's Industry Surveys**
www.standardpoor.com

56. **Streamline** (produced by Informit Online)
www.informit.com.au

57. **Superior Information Services**
www.superiorinfo.com/index.html

58. **Wall Street Transcript**
www.twst.com

59. **WEFA**
www.wefa.com

60. **Yahoo!**
www.yahoo.com

# Electronic Discussion Groups, Mailing Lists and Electronic Newsletters

61. **AIIP-L**
Available to AIIP members only
www.aiip.org

62. **American Association of Law Libraries**
www.aallnet.org/discuss/list_gateway.asp

63. **Buslib-L**
To subscribe, send email to:
listserv@listserv.boisestate.edu
In message body type:
subscribe buslib-l firstname lastname

64. **Outsell's E-brief**
To subscribe, send email to:
dcurle@outsellinc.com
In message body list your name, preferred email address, job title and a brief description of how you heard about E-brief, for a free 2-month trial subscription. Yearly fee is $395 for an individual subscription.

65. **Search Engine Watch**
www.searchenginewatch.com

66. **SLA Advertising Division**
To subscribe, send email to:
listserv@ listserv.sla.org
In message body type:
subscribe SLA-DAM firstname lastname

67. **SLA Business & Finance Division**
    To subscribe, send email to:
    listserv@lists.psu.eduin
    In message body type:
    subscribe SLABF-L firstname lastname

68. **SLA Communications Division**
    To subscribe, email
    listserv@listserv.sla.org
    In message body type:
    subscribe SLA-DCOM firstname lastname

69. **SLA Consultants Section,
    Library Management Division**
    To subscribe, send email to:
    listserv@psuvm.psu.edu
    In message body type:
    subscribe LMDSLA-L firstname lastname

70. **SLA Information Technology Division**
    To subscribe, send email to:
    listserv@listserv.sla.org
    In message body type:
    subscribe SLA-DITE firstname lastname

71. **SLA Legal Division**
    To subscribe, send email to:
    majordomo@albertus.lawlib.uh.edu
    In message body type:
    subscribe SLA-LAW YourEmailAddress

72. **Stumpers-L**
    To subscribe, send email to:
    mailserv@cuis.edu
    In message body type:
    subscribe STUMPERS-L YourEmailAddress

73. **Tax Librarians**
    To subscribe, send email to:
    majordomo@lists.tax.org
    In message body type:
    subscribe TAX-LIBRARIANS YourEmailAddress

## Other Resources

74. **Association of Independent
    Information Professionals** (AIIP)
    www.aiip.org

75. **Brill's Content**
Brill Media Ventures, New York, NY, 10x/year
www.brillscontent.com

76. **CyberSkeptic's Guide to Internet Research**
BiblioData, Needham Heights, MA, 10x/year
www.bibliodata.com

77. **Database**
Online, Inc., Wilton, CT, bimonthly
www.onlineinc.com/database

78. **Encyclopedia of Associations**
Gale Research, Farmington Hills, MI, 1998

79. **Encyclopedia of Business Information Sources**
Gale Research, Farmington Hills, MI, 1998

80. **Find It Fast:**
**How to Uncover Expert Information on Any Subject**
HarperCollins, New York, NY 1997

81. **Finding Business Research on the Web**
Find/SVP, New York, NY, 1997
www.findsvp.com

82. **Find It Online!**
Windcrest/McGraw-Hill
New York, 1994

83. **Fulltext Sources Online**
Information Today, Inc., Medford, NJ, semi-annually
www.infotoday.com

84. **Industry Standard**
The Industry Standard, San Francisco, CA, weekly
www.thestandard.net

85. **InfoAlert**
*[Editor's note: discontinued publication since interview.]*

86. **Information Advisor**
Find/SVP, New York, monthly
www.findsvp.com

87. **Information Outlook**
Special Libraries Association, Washington, DC, monthly
InformationOutlook.com

88. **Information Today**
Information Today, Inc., Medford, NJ, monthly
www.infotoday.com/it/itnew.htm

89. **Information World Review: Learned Information**
Oxford, U.K., monthly
www.iwr.co.uk/iwr

90. *Internet Connection*
    Bernan Press, Washington, DC, 10x/year
    www.bernan.com

91. **Notess, Greg**
    www.notess.com/search

92. *Online*
    Online, Inc., Wilton, CT, bimonthly
    www.onlineinc.com/onlinemag

93. *Online Currents*
    Enterprise Information, Sydney, Australia, 10x/year
    www.sofcom.com.au/olc

94. *Searcher*
    Information Today, Inc., Medford, NJ, 10x/year.
    www.infotoday.com/searcher

95. *SI*: *Special Issues*
    Reference Press, Austin, TX, annual, with monthly updates

96. **Society of Competitive Intelligence Professionals** (SCIP)
    www.scip.org

97. **Southern California Association of Law Libraries** (SCALL)
    www.aallnet.org/chapter/scall

98. **Southern California Online Users Group** (SCOUG)
    www.scougweb.org

99. **Special Libraries Association** (SLA)
    www.sla.org

100. *U.S. Industry & Trade Outlook*
     www.ita.doc.gov/td/industry/otea/usito99/index.htm
     U.S. Department of Commerce, Washington, DC, 1998
     www.ita.doc.gov/outlook

101. *Yahoo! Internet Life*
     www.zdnet.com/yil

# Appendix B:
## Glossary

**10-K.** The annual report that most publicly traded companies file with the U.S. Securities and Exchange Commission.

**AIIP.** Association of Independent Information Professionals. An international association of people who own their own information businesses. www.aiip.org

**Bookmark.** A Web browser feature that lets you store a link to a Web site, enabling you to return to the site later. Internet Explorer calls bookmarks "Favorite Web Sites."

**CI.** Competitive Intelligence. Collecting and analyzing information about industry developments and market trends, particularly of a company's competitors.

**EDGAR.** Electronic Data Gathering, Analysis, and Retrieval. The system within the U.S. Securities and Exchange Commission that collects electronic filings and makes them available on the Net. edgar.sec.gov

**GUI.** Graphical User Interface, which enables you to use a mouse, trackball or other device to "point and click."

**HTML.** Hyper Text Markup Language. The coding scheme used for designing and displaying documents on the Web.

**ISP.** Internet Service Provider

**LISTSERV.** The trademarked name of one of the predominant electronic mailing list management systems. Note that "listserv" is often used as a generic term for any electronic discussion group, whether run on LISTSERV or another software package. www.lsoft.com/listserv.stm

**M.L.I.S. or M.L.S.** Master's in Library (and Information) Studies. The graduate degree earned by many librarians and information professionals.

**Newsgroup.** An Internet-based topical discussion area, generally part of the Usenet hierarchy.

**PDF.** Adobe Portable Document Format. This allows the electronic dissemination of documents with their original format, including images and layout, intact. www.adobe.com/prodindex/acrobat/adobepdf.html

**Professional Online Service.** Value-added online information system designed for professional researchers. Dialog, Dow Jones Interactive and Lexis-Nexis are three leading professional online services.

**Search Engine.** A software tool that indexes Web pages or online databases and allows users to search by words and URLs. Most search engines attempt to include as many Web pages as possible. See also **Web Catalog**.

**SEC.** U.S. Securities and Exchange Commission. www.sec.gov

**SLA.** Special Libraries Association. www.sla.org

**URL.** Uniform Resource Locator. The address of a Web page or other Internet resource.

**Usenet.** A collection of thousands of newsgroups, plus the computers that host them and the user population that participates in them.

**Web Catalog.** A Web site that selectively indexes Web pages and allows users to browse the index by category or search by words or URLs. Most Web catalogs are intentionally far from comprehensive in their coverage. See also **Search Engine**.

# Index:

# About the Author

Mary Ellen Bates is the owner of Bates Information Services, providing business research to business professionals and corporate librarians. Prior to starting her own company in 1992, she worked in corporate and law libraries for fifteen years. She received her Masters in Library and Information Science from the University of California, Berkeley and has been an online researcher in libraries and information centers since the late 1970s.

She is the author of *The Online Deskbook* (Information Today, Inc., 1996), writes Bates' Back Page for *Database* magazine and has written extensively about the online world. She has been an invited speaker at information industry conferences in the U.S., Mexico, Germany, Denmark and Sweden. She is a past president of the Association of Independent Information Professionals and is active in the Special Libraries Association.

She lives in Washington, DC, with her companion and her dog. She can be contacted at mbates@BatesInfo.com.

# About the Editor

Reva Basch, executive editor of the Super Searchers series, is a writer, researcher and consultant to the online industry. She is author of the original Super Searcher books, *Secrets of the Super Searchers* and *Secrets of the Super Net Searchers*, as well as *Researching Online For Dummies* and *Electronic Information Delivery: Ensuring Quality and Value*. She writes the Reva's (W)rap column for *ONLINE* magazine, has contributed numerous articles and columns to professional journals and the popular press, and has keynoted at conferences in Europe, Scandinavia, Australia, Canada and the U.S.

A past president of the Association of Independent Information Professionals, she has a Master's in Library Science from the University of California at Berkeley, and more than 20 years of experience in database and Internet research. Reva was Vice President and Director of Research at Information on Demand and has been president of her own company, Aubergine Information Services, since 1986.

She lives with her husband and three cats on the Northern California coast.

# More CyberAge Books from Information Today, Inc.

## LAW OF THE SUPER SEARCHERS
### The Online Secrets of Top Legal Researchers
**T. R. Halvorson • Edited by Reva Basch**

With lives and fortunes depending on it, the integrity and timeliness of legal research is critical. In *Law of the Super Searchers*, practicing attorney and online searcher T. R. Halvorson gets eight leading legal researchers to reveal their personal strategies for successful online searching. Here, for the first time, these experts share insider tips, techniques, and hard-won knowledge—guaranteed to help any legal researcher use the Internet and online services to find and evaluate the information they need.

**Softbound • ISBN 0-910965-34-X • $24.95**

## SECRETS OF THE SUPER NET SEARCHERS
### The Reflections, Revelations and Hard-Won Wisdom of 35 of the World's Top Internet Researchers
**Reva Basch • Edited by Mary Ellen Bates**

Reva Basch, whom *WIRED* Magazine has called "The Ultimate Intelligent Agent," delivers insights, anecdotes, tips, techniques, and case studies through her interviews with 35 of the world's top Internet hunters and gatherers. The Super Net Searchers explain how to find valuable information on the Internet, distinguish cyber-gems from cyber-junk, avoid "Internet Overload," and much more.

**Softbound • ISBN 0-910965-22-6 • $29.95**

## DESIGN WISE
### A Guide for Evaluating the Interface Design of Information Resources
**Alison Head**

"*Design Wise* takes us beyond what's cool and what's hot and shows us what works and what doesn't."

—Elizabeth Osder, *The New York Times on the Web*

The increased usage of computers and the Internet for accessing information has resulted in a torrent of new multimedia products. For an information user, the question used to be: "What's the name of the provider that carries so-and-so?" Today, the question is: "Of all the versions of so-and-so, which one is the easiest to use?" The result is that knowing how to size up user-centered interface design is becoming as important for people who choose and use information resources as for those who design them. *Design Wise* introduces readers to the basics of interface design, and explains why and how a design evaluation should be undertaken before you buy or license Web- and disk-based information products.

**Softbound • ISBN 0-910965-31-5 • $29.95**